Cancerians are good at keeping their emotions out of public
– Astrology Enthusiast

THIS ART BOOK IS SPECIALLY DESIGNED FOR THE PEOPLE IN CANCER ZODIAC SIGN.
IT HAS 24 PAGES OF TAURUS BASED SKETCH.

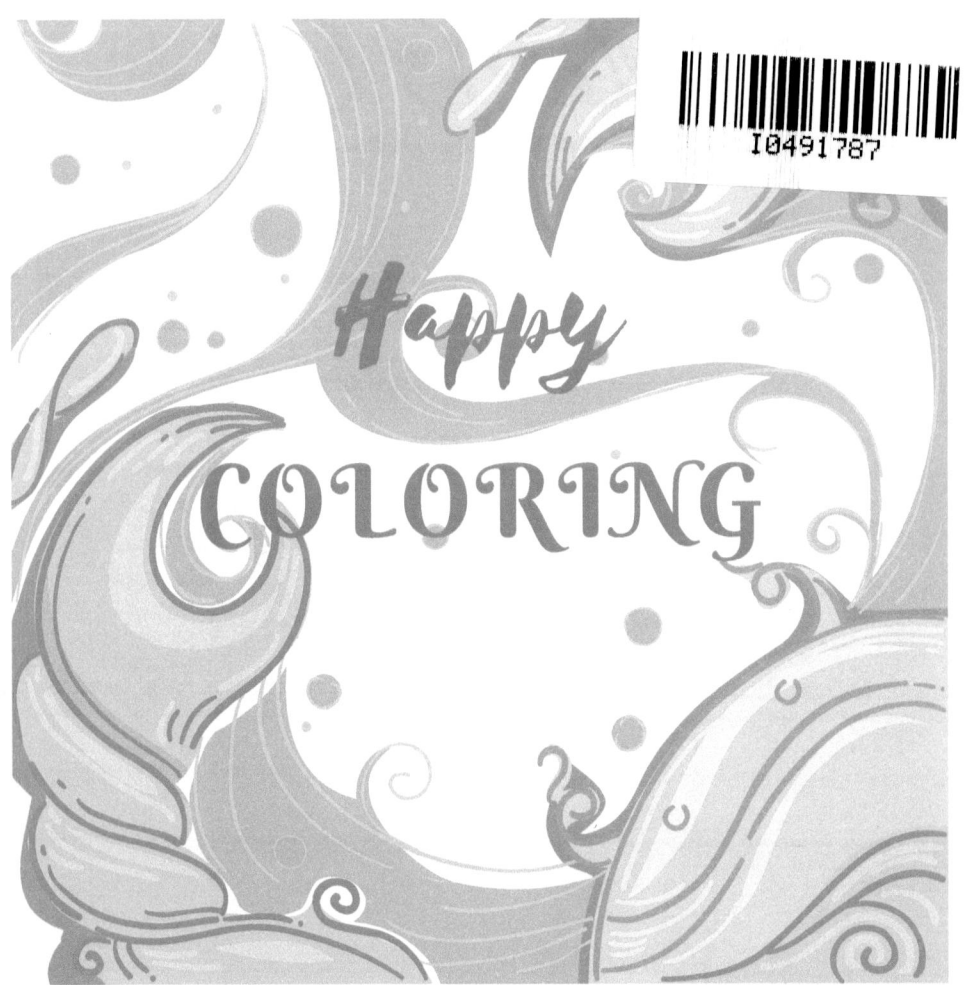

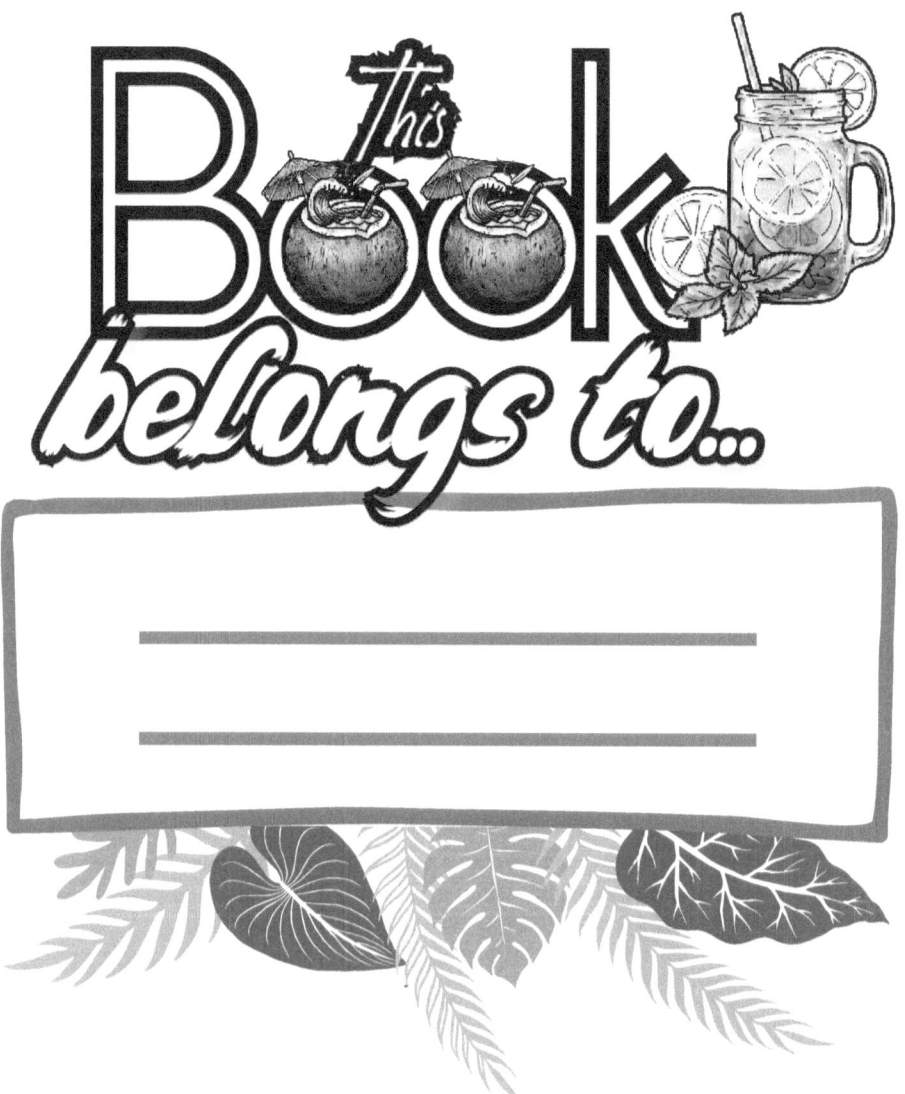

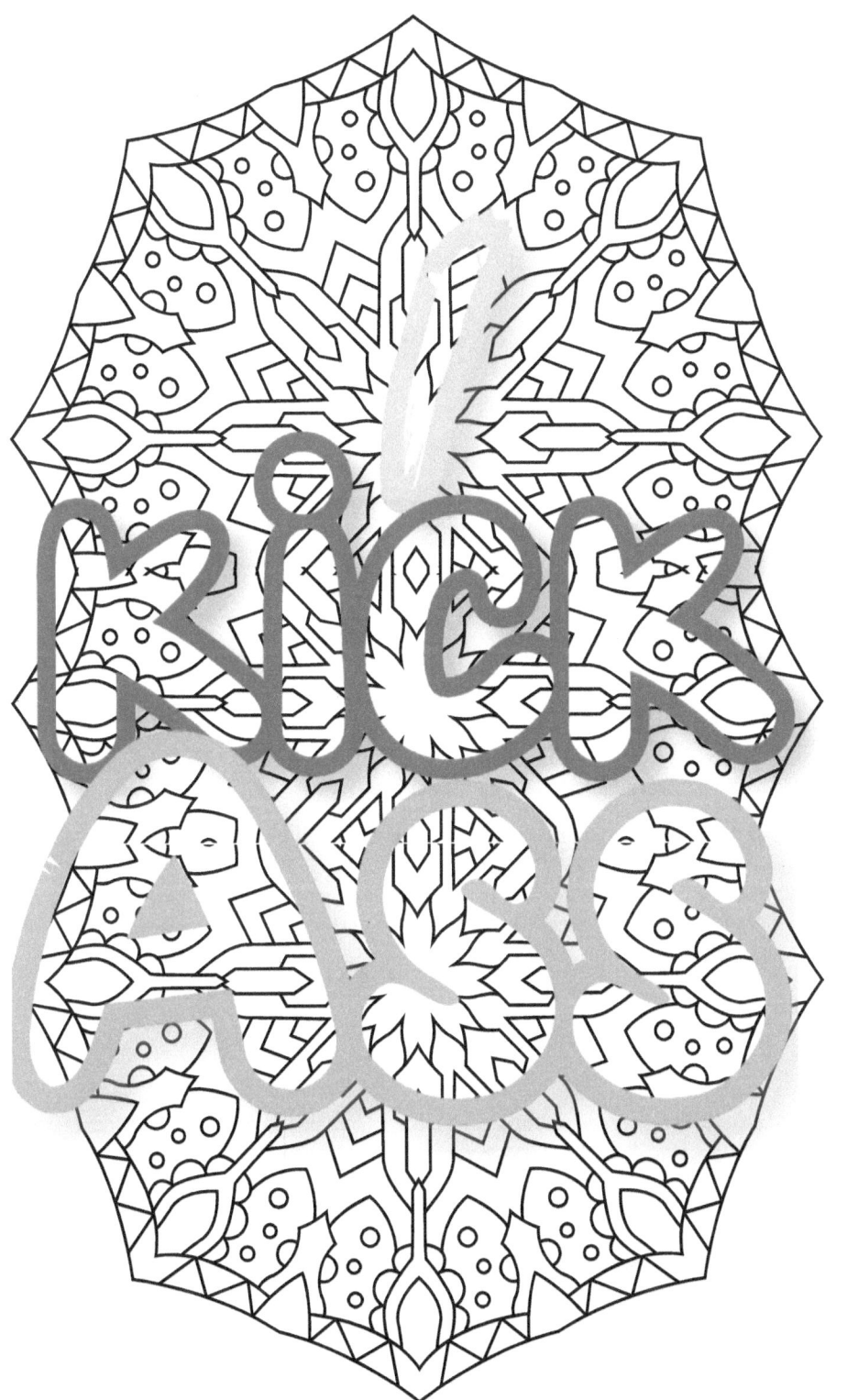

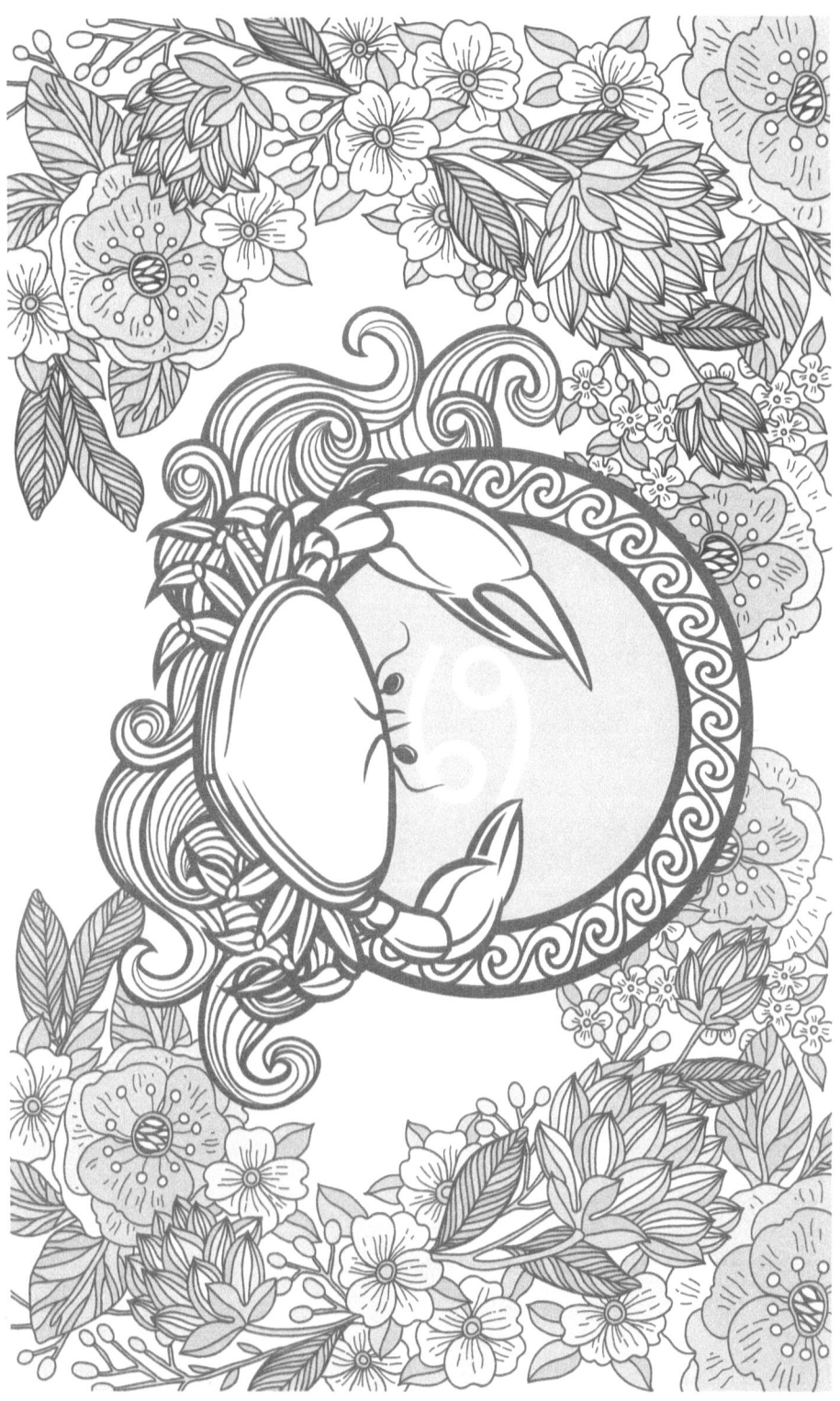

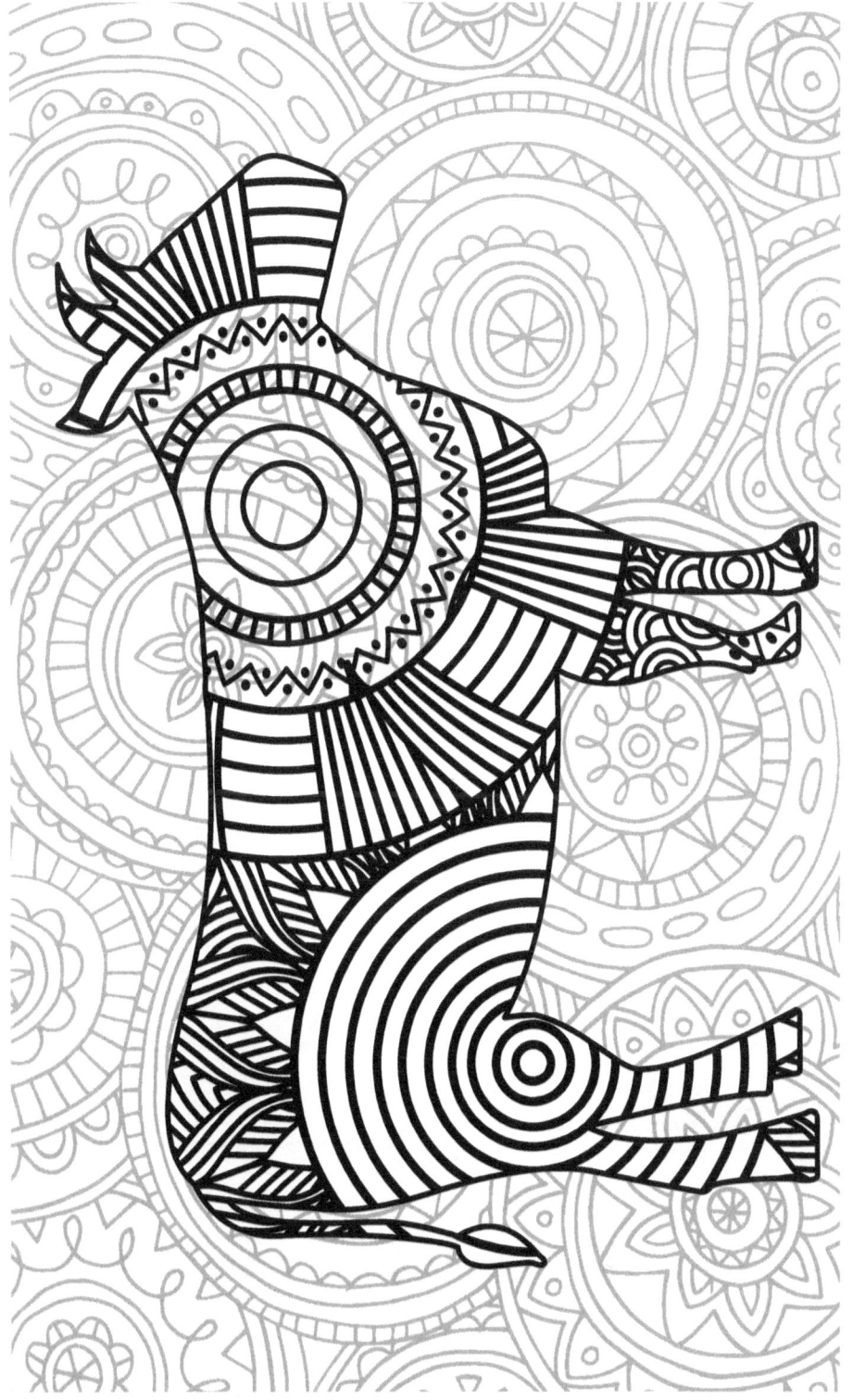

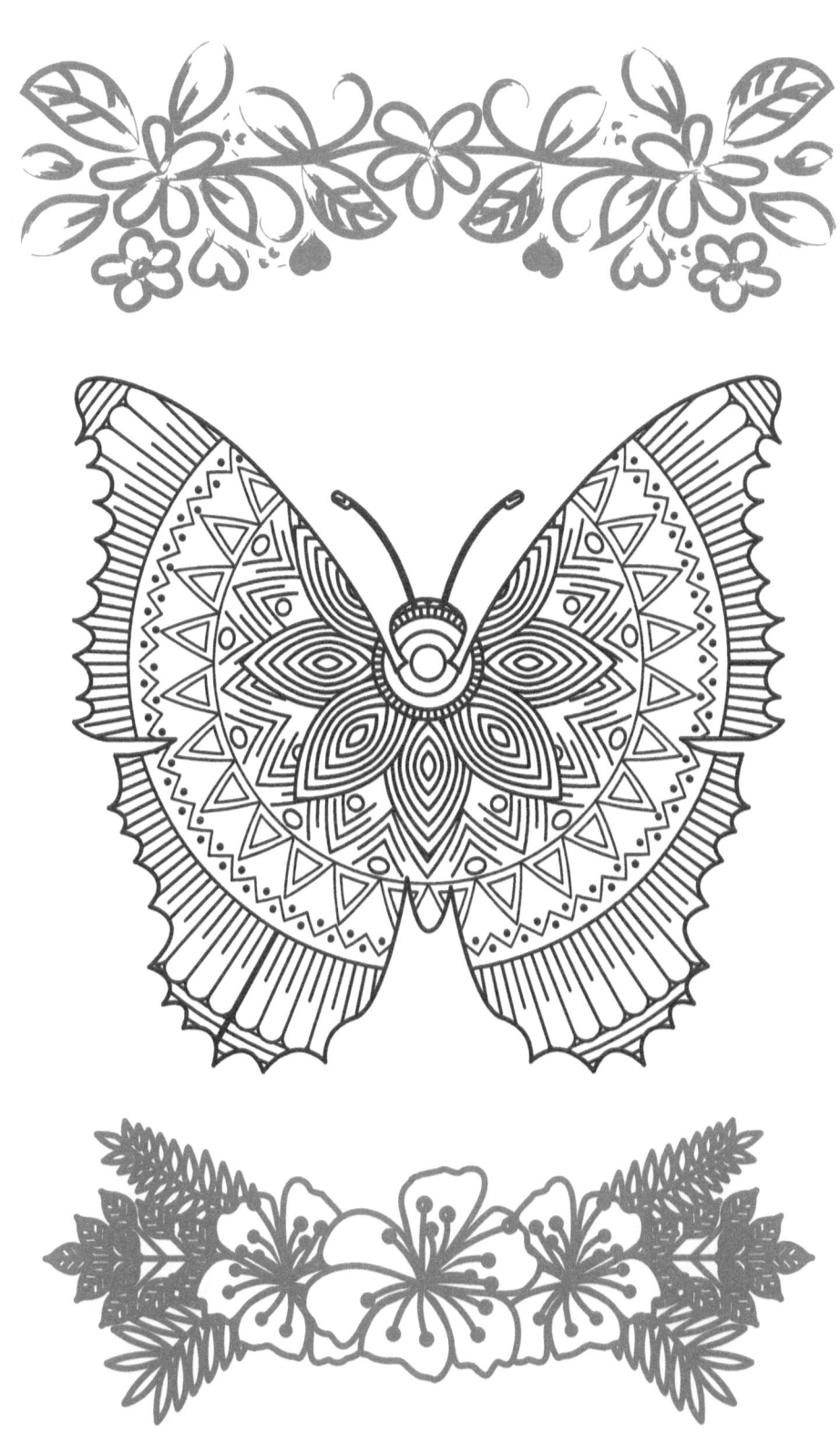

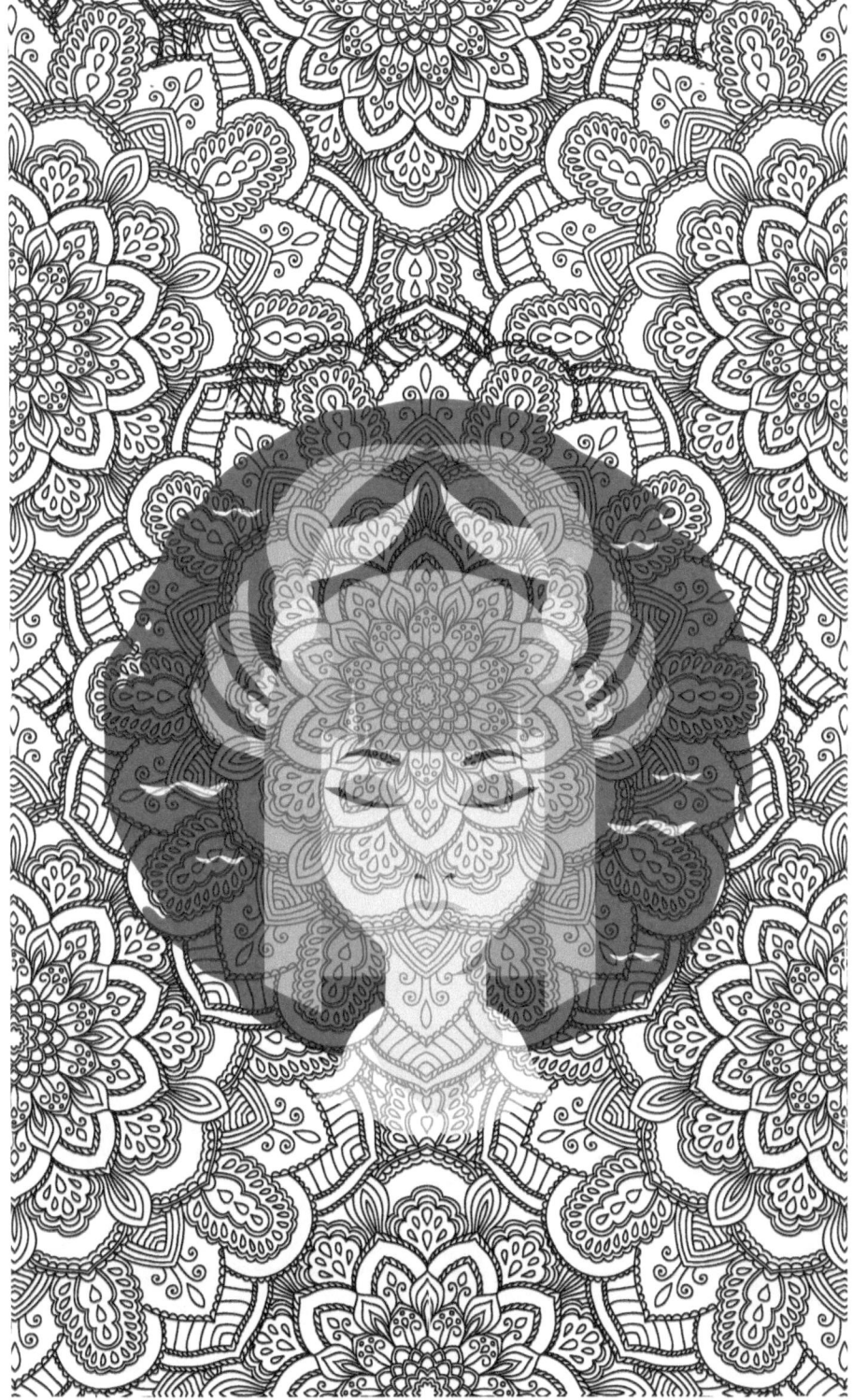

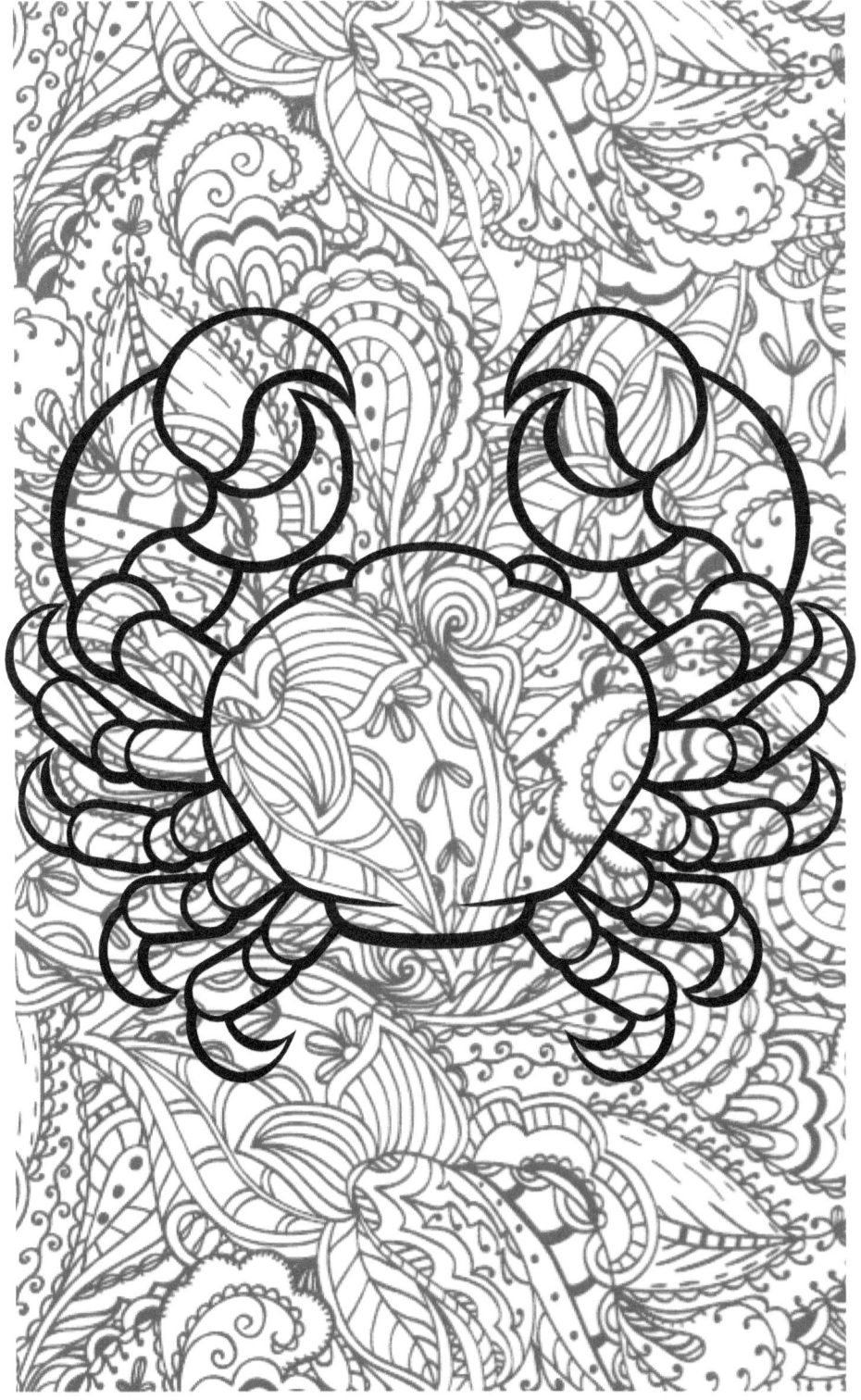

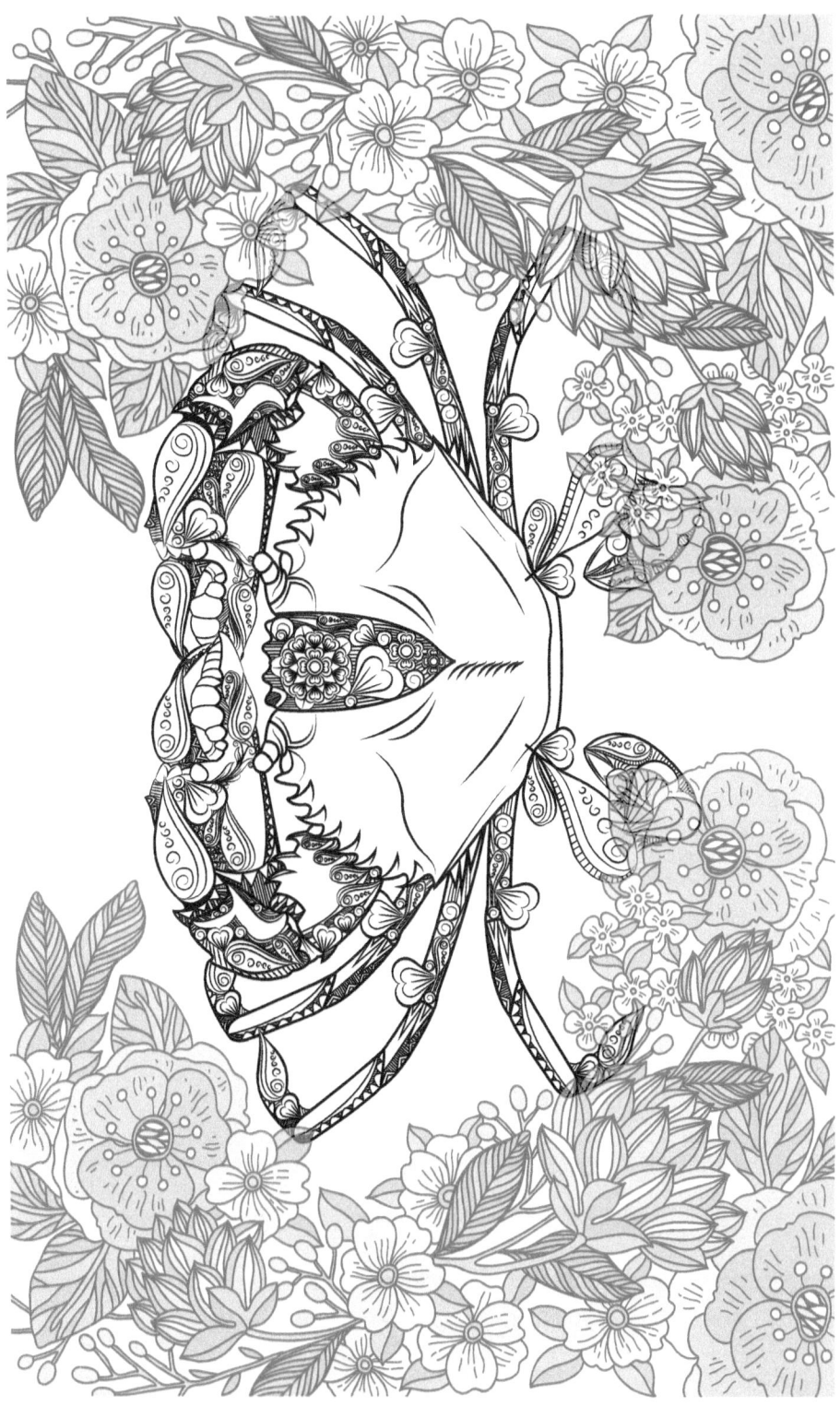

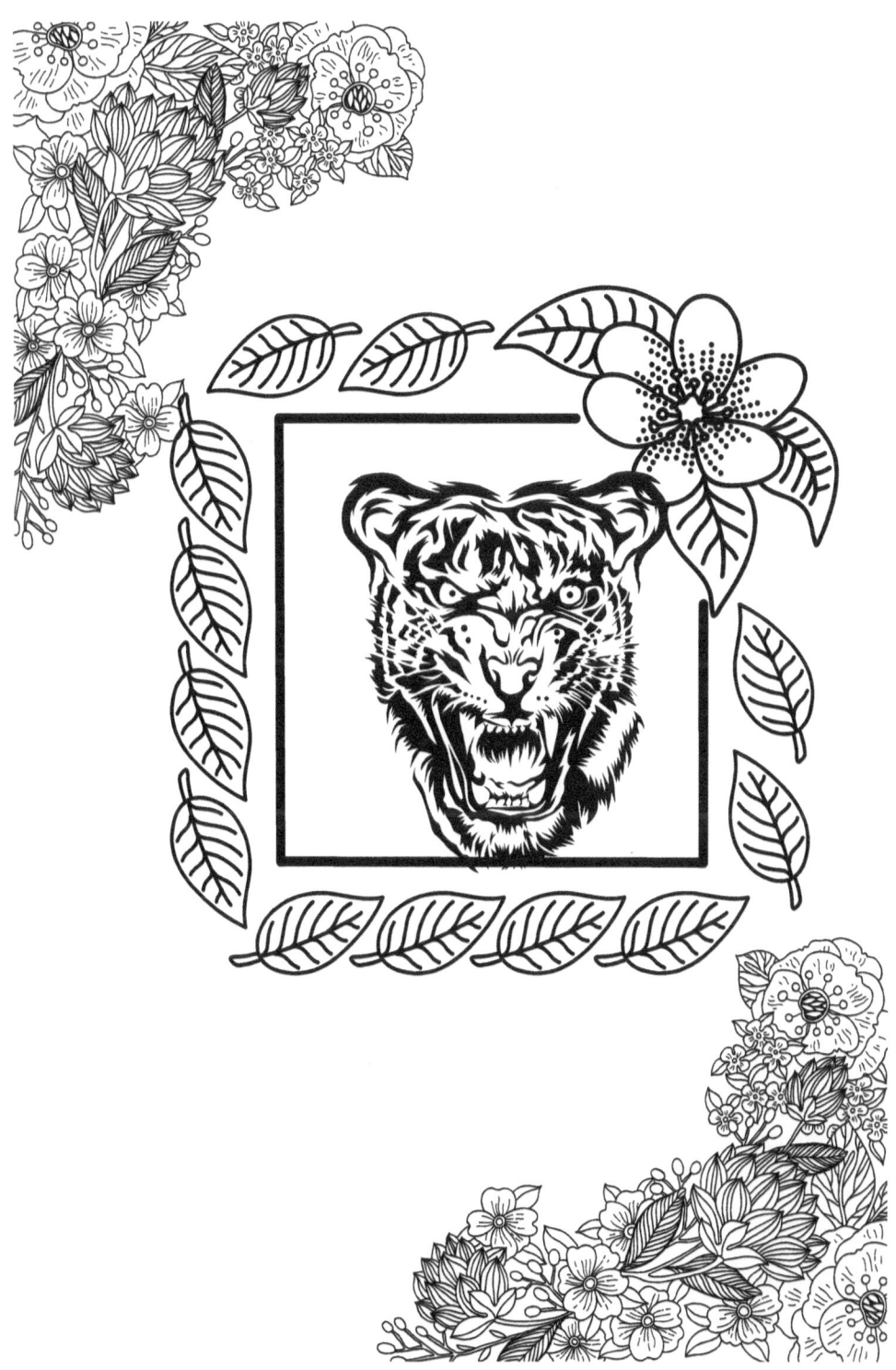

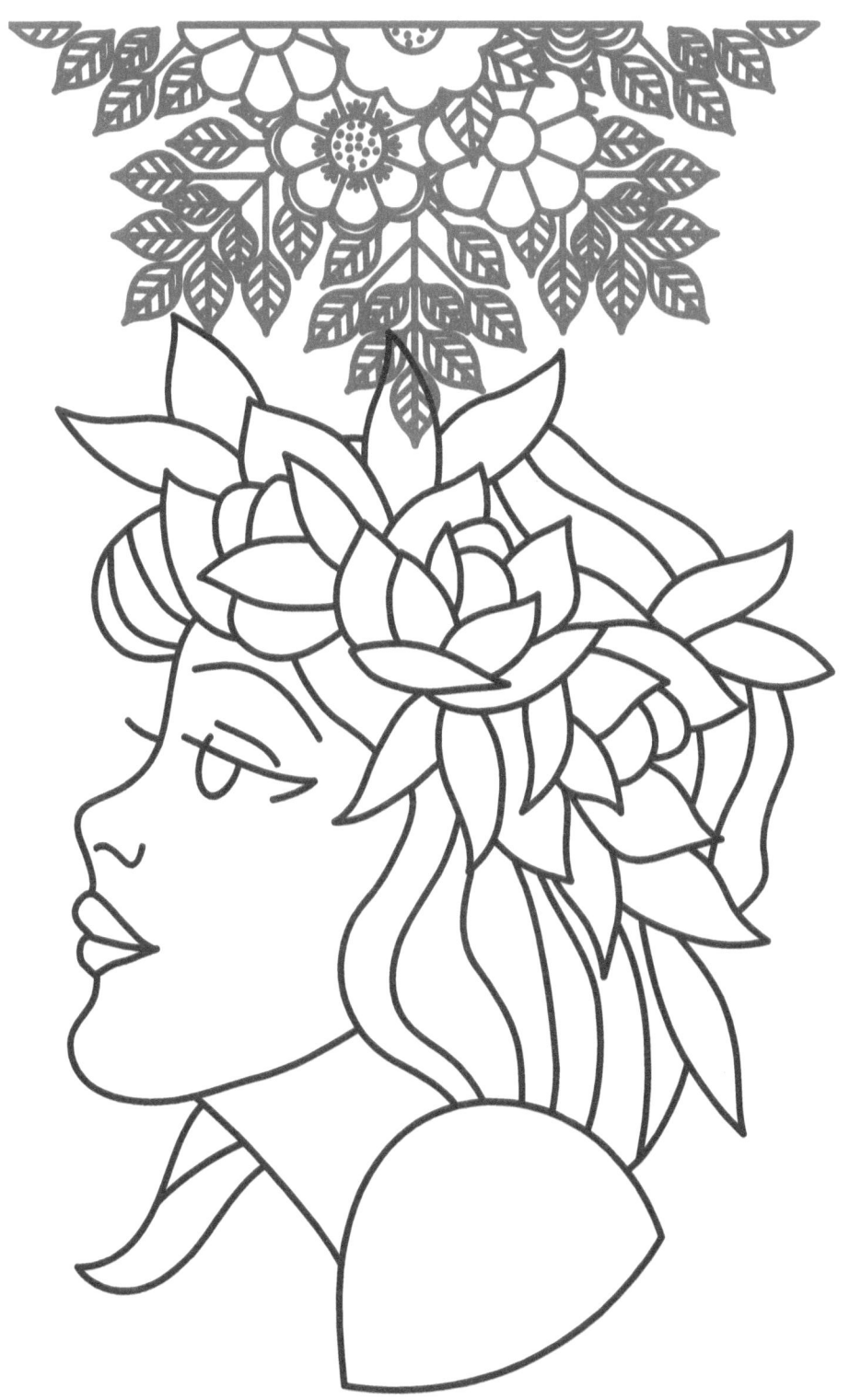

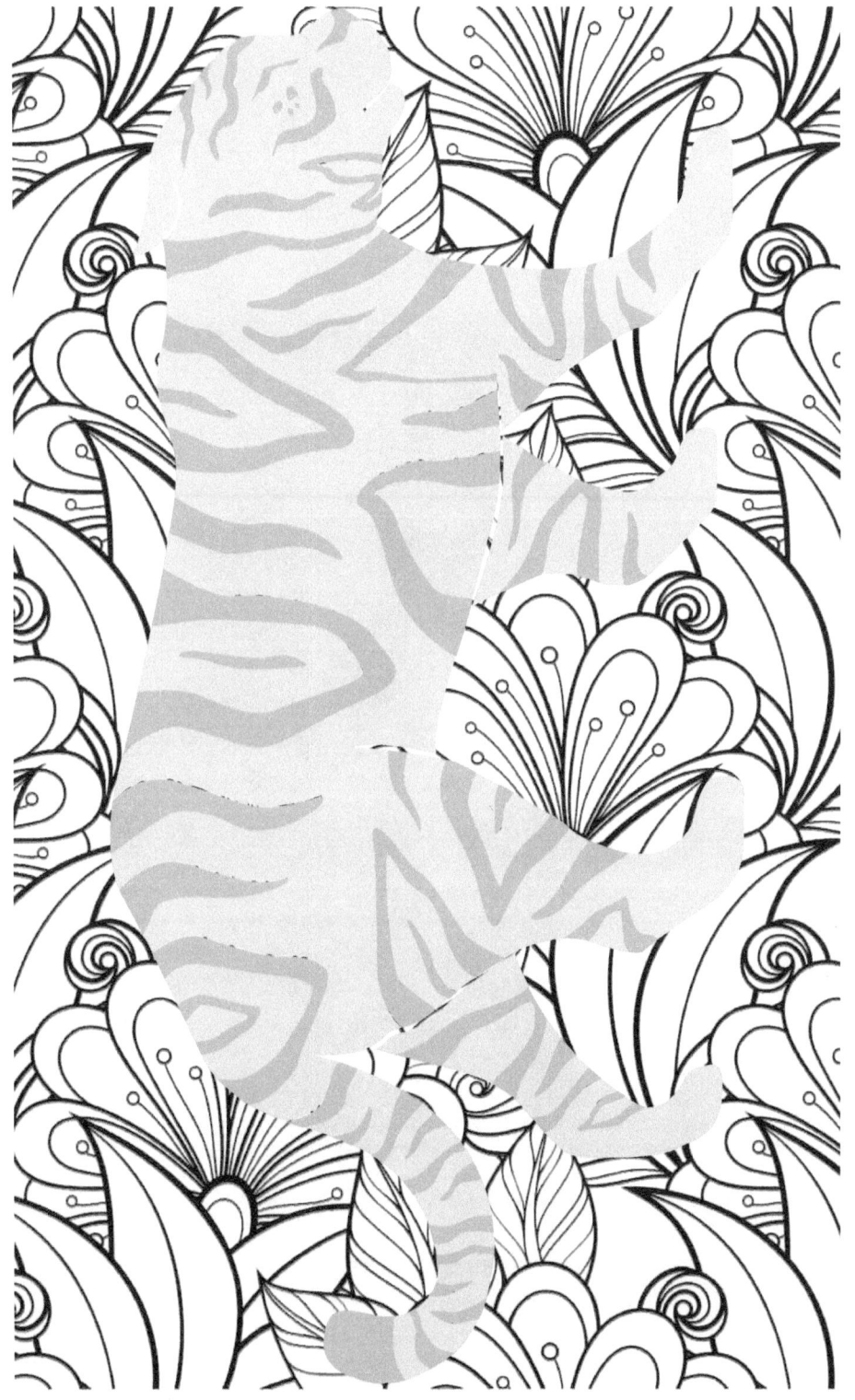

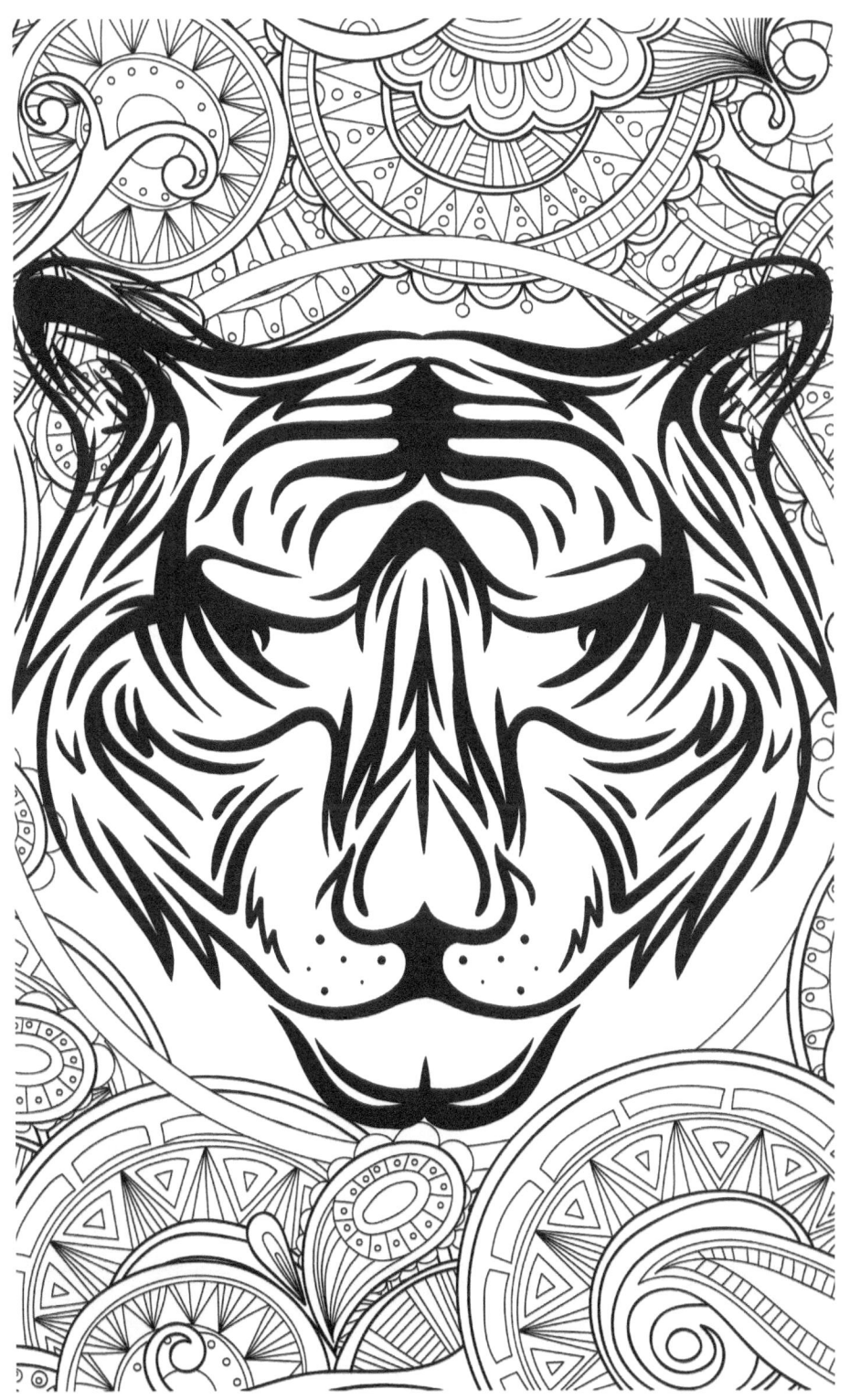

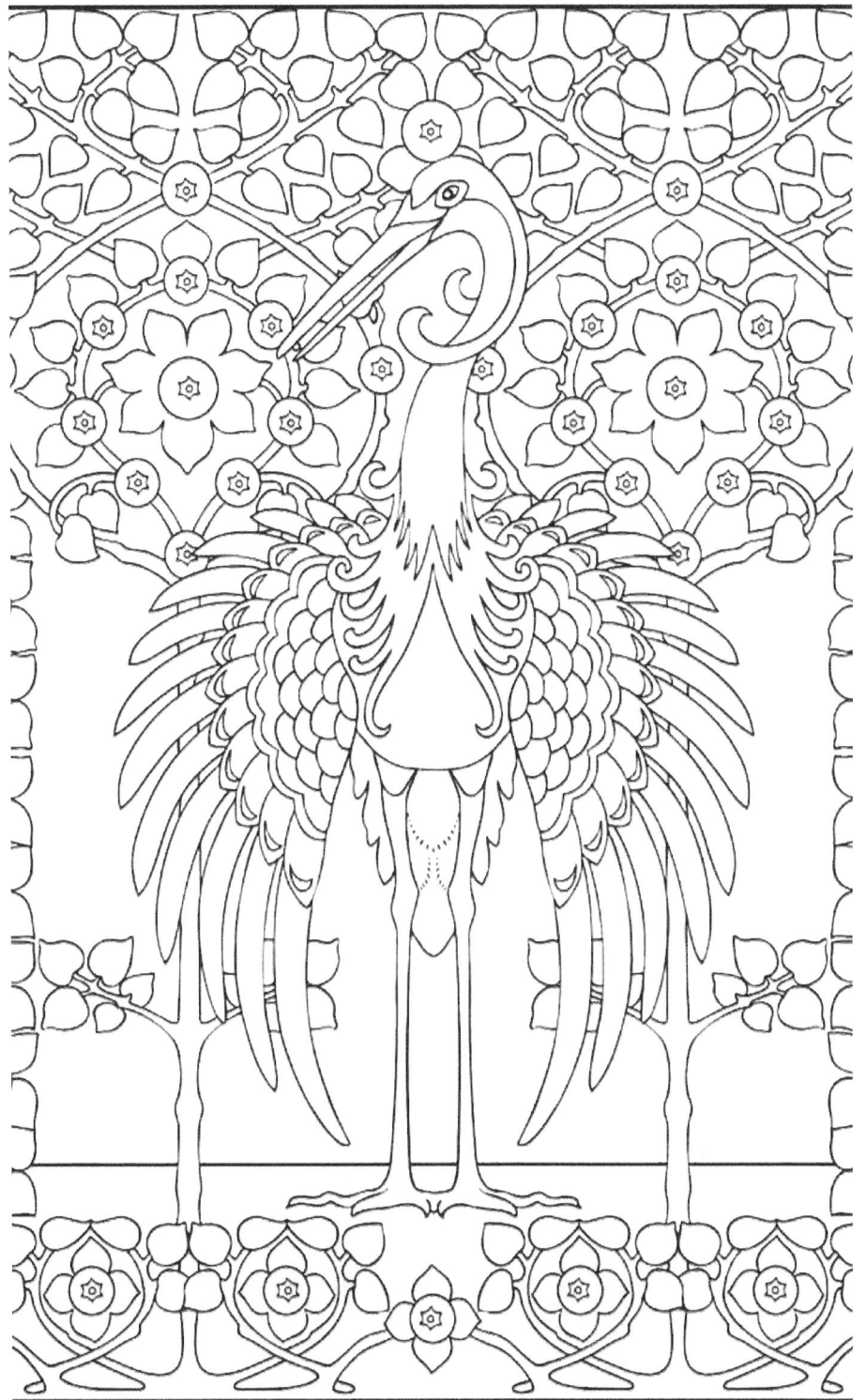

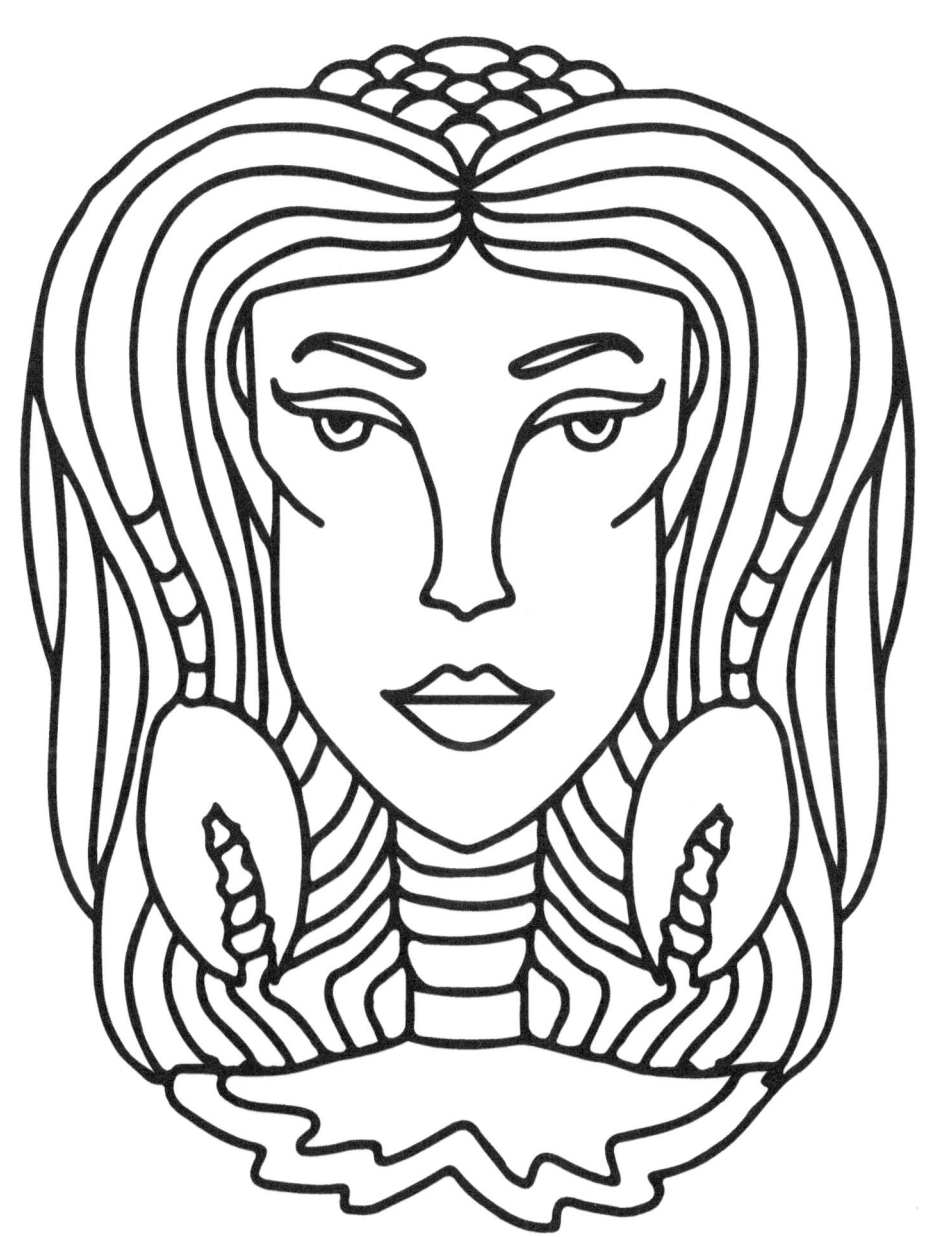

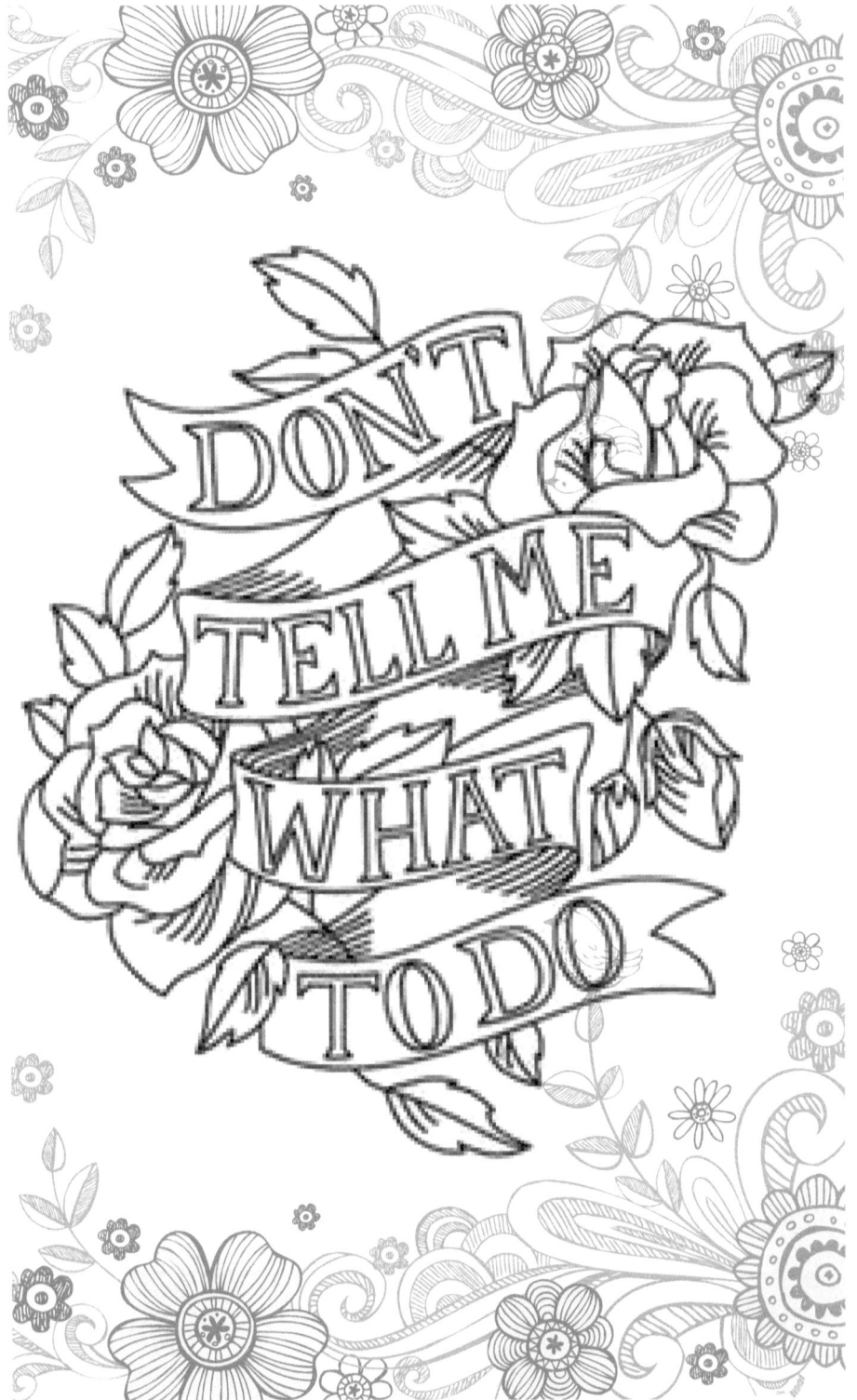

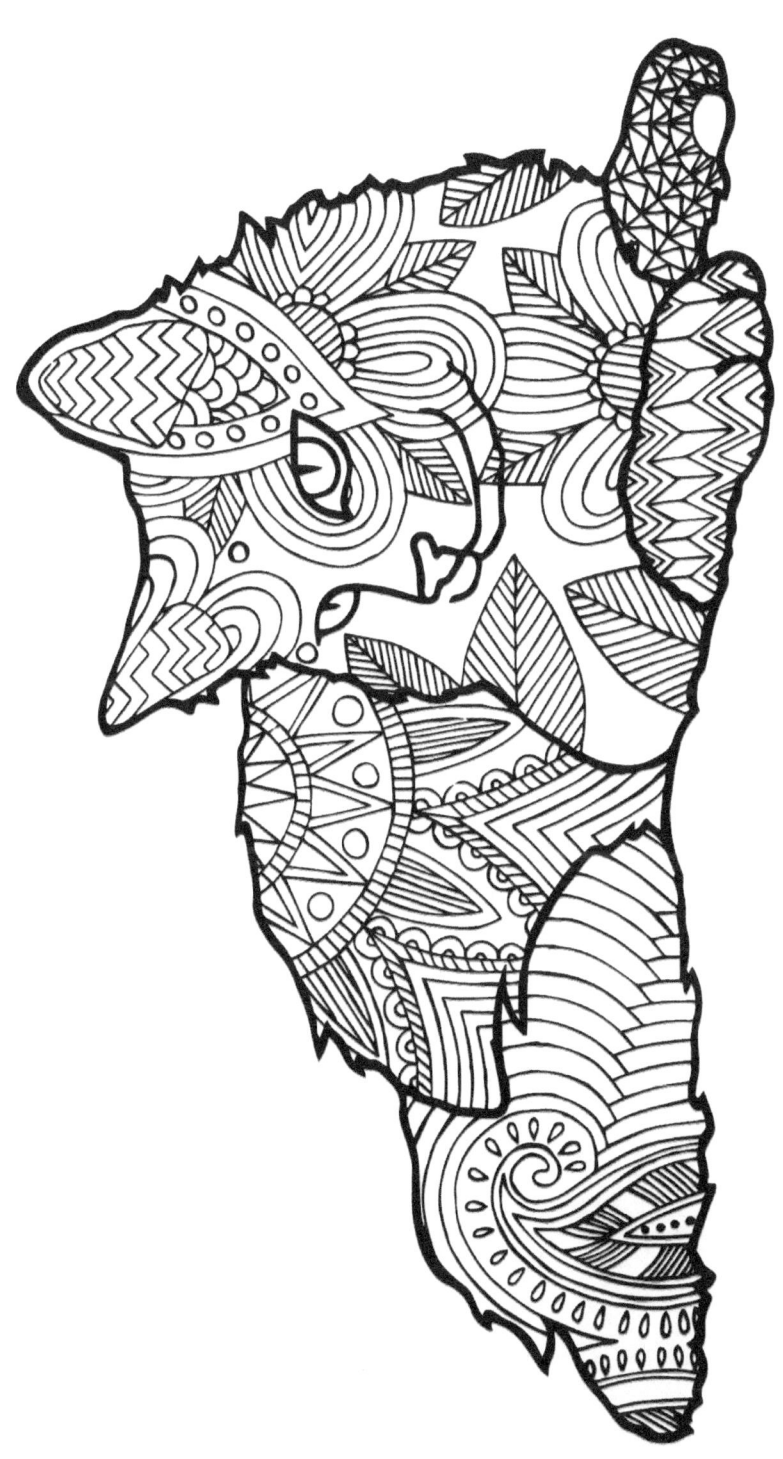

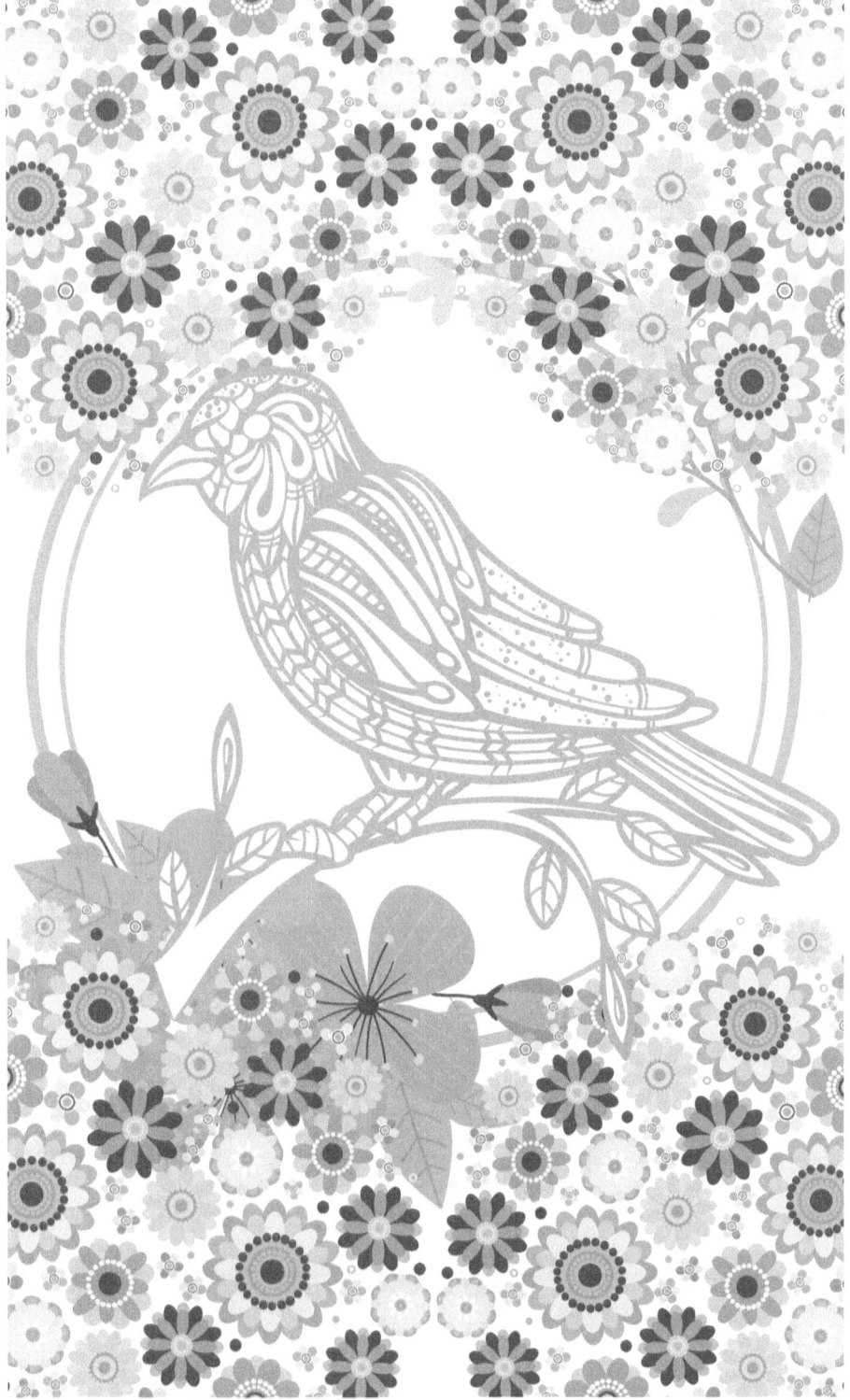

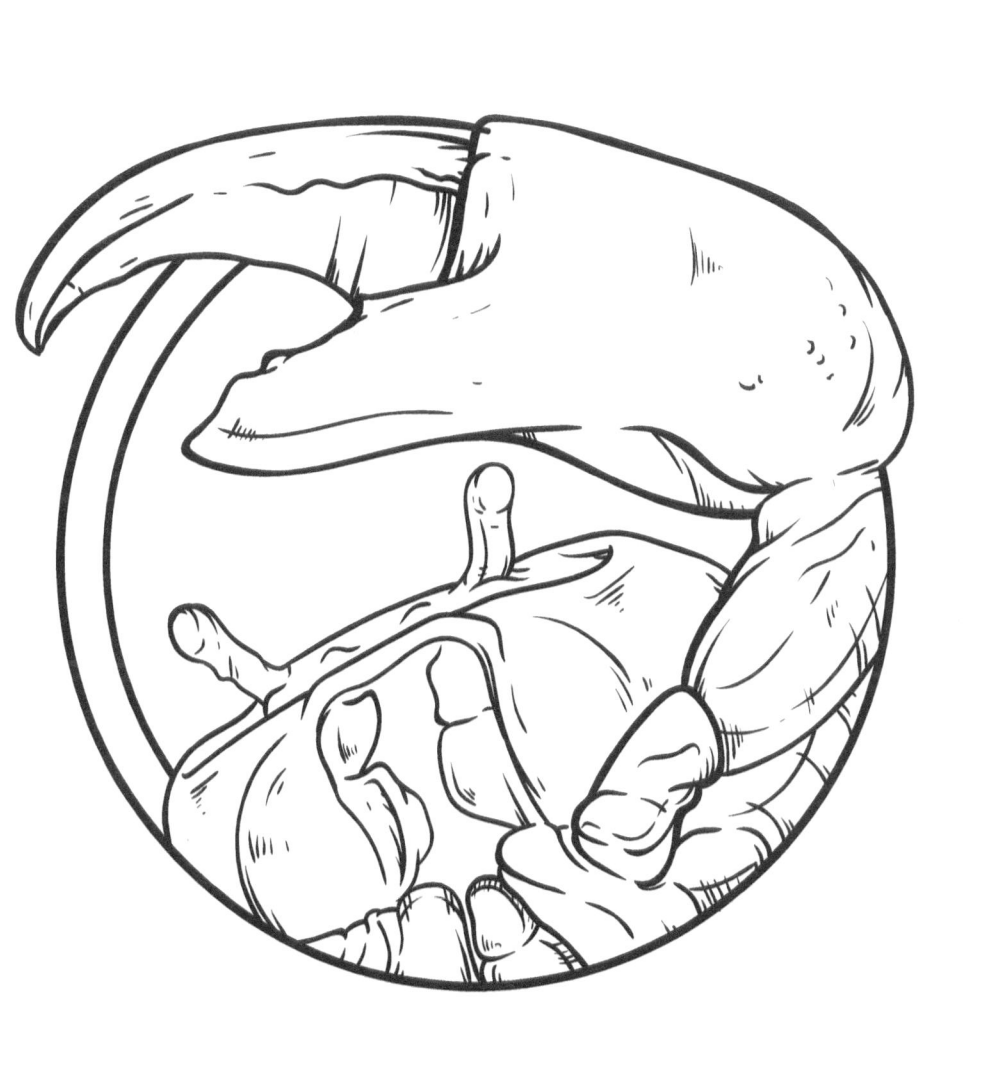

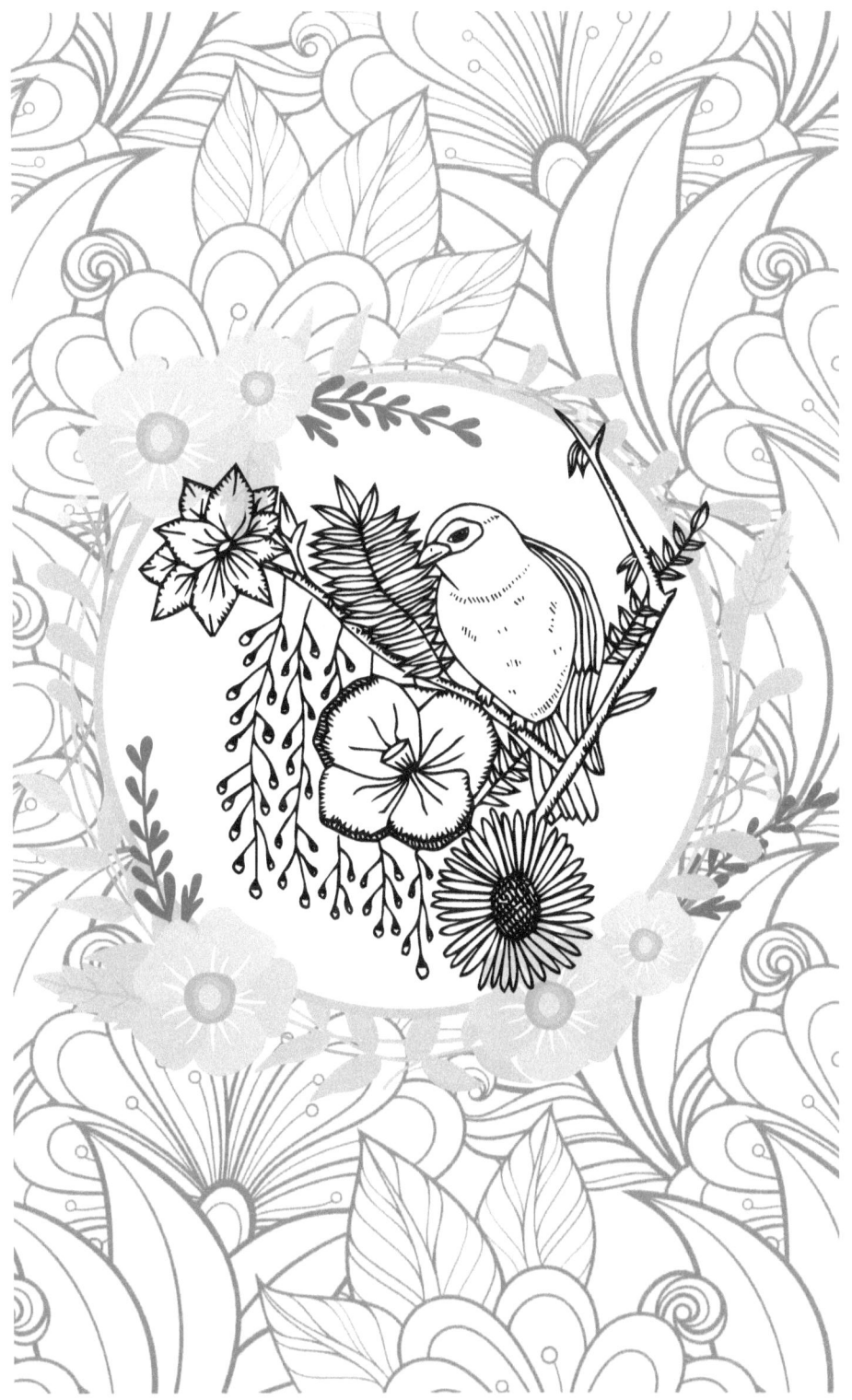

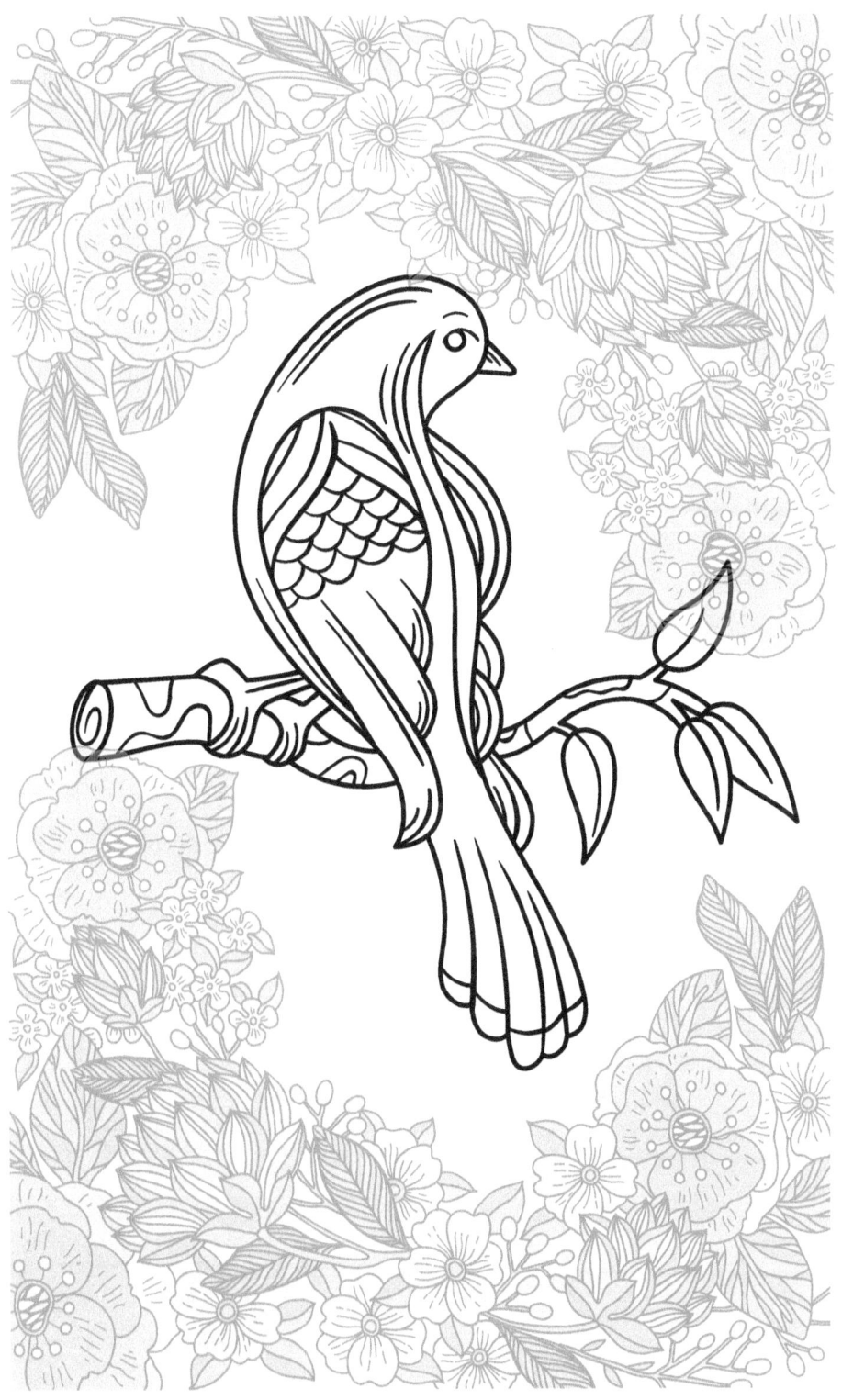

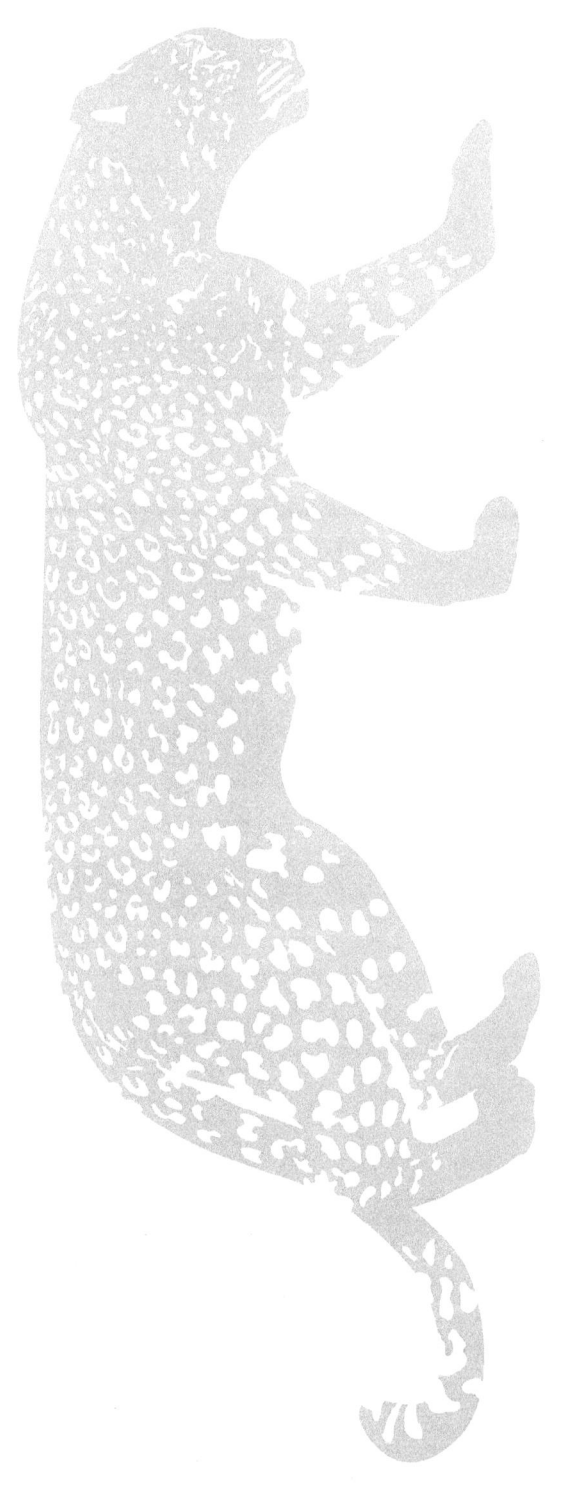

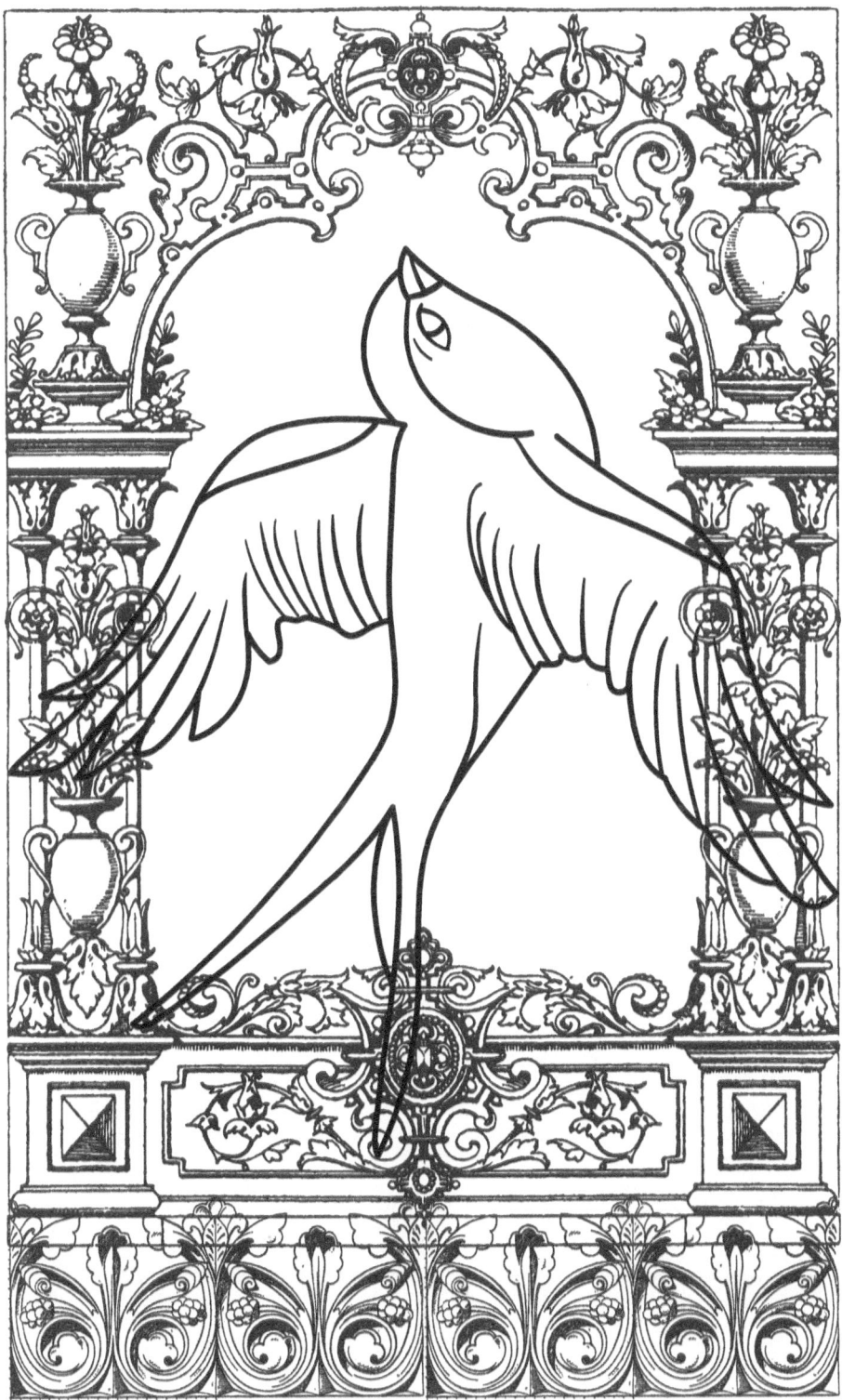

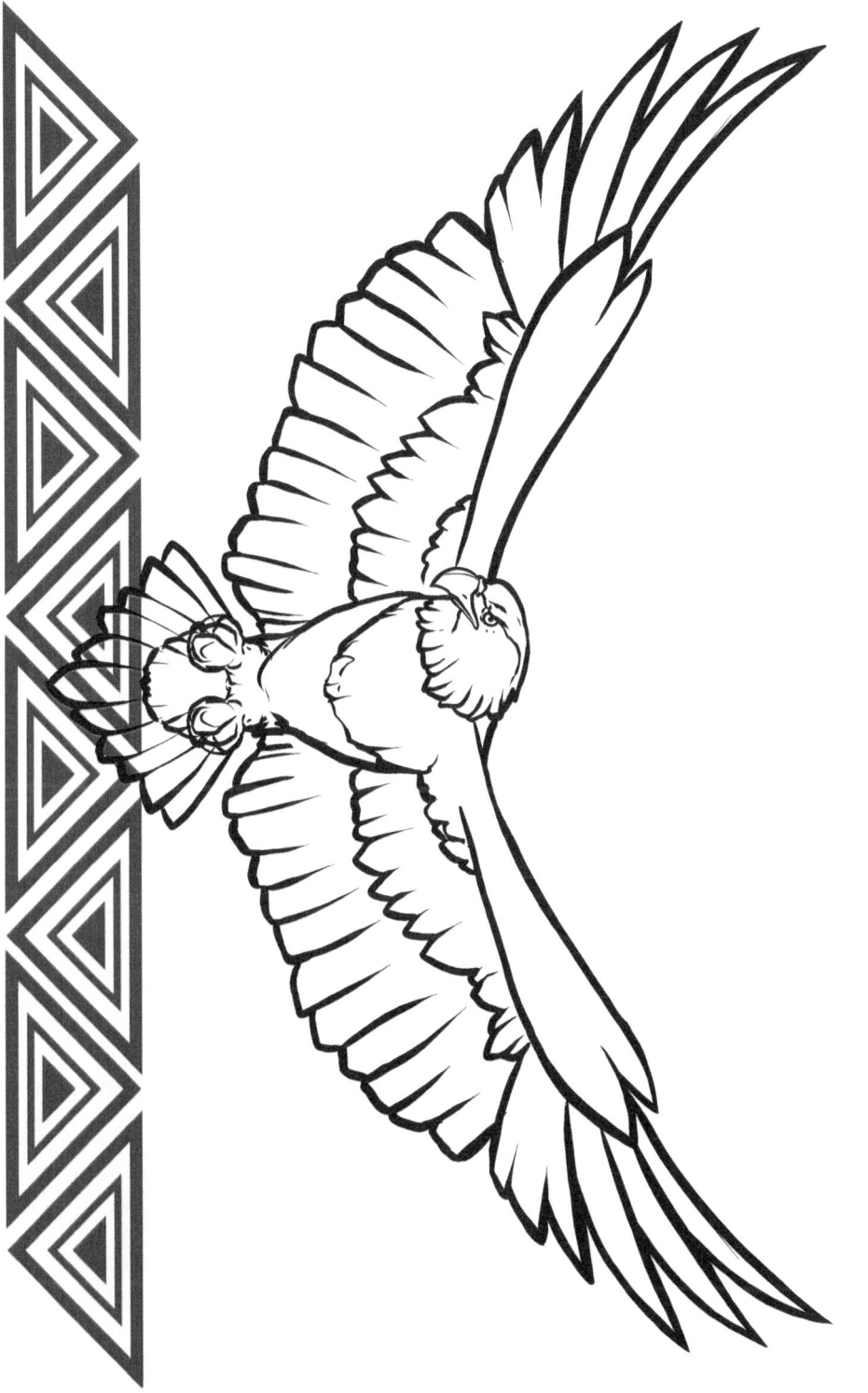

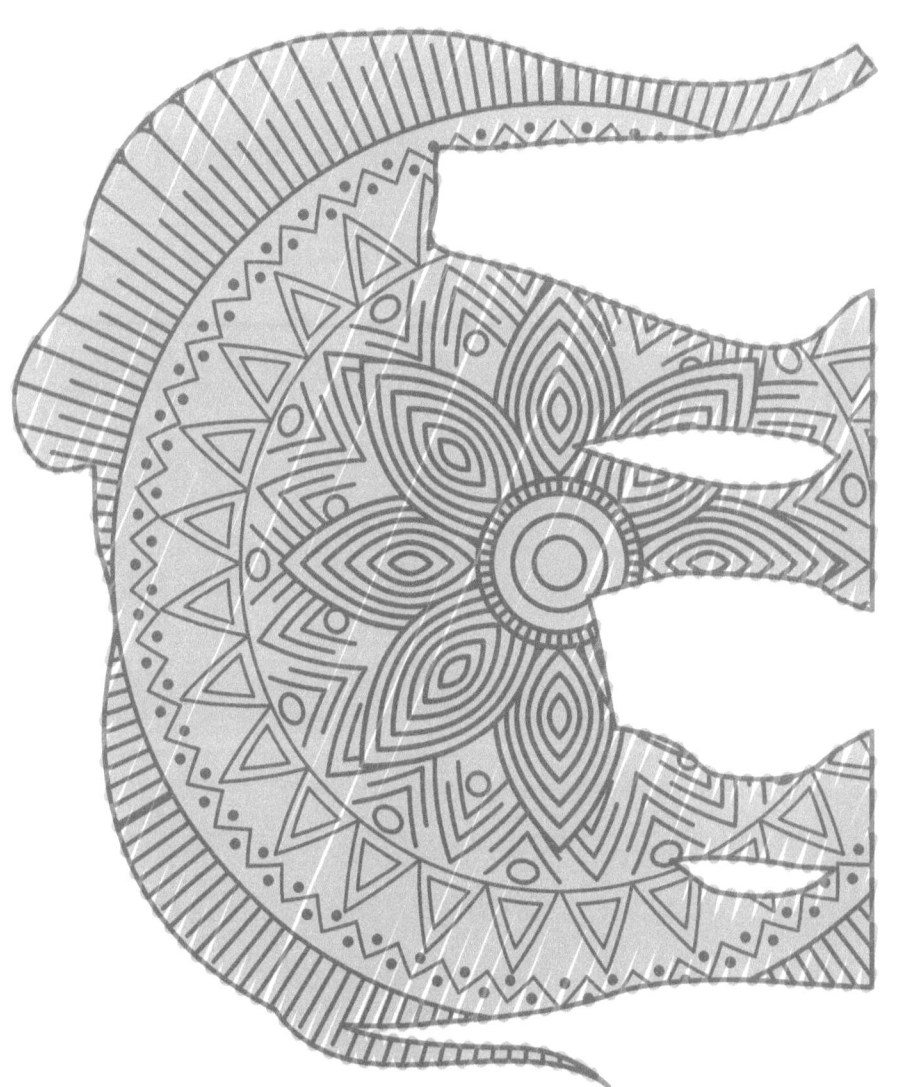

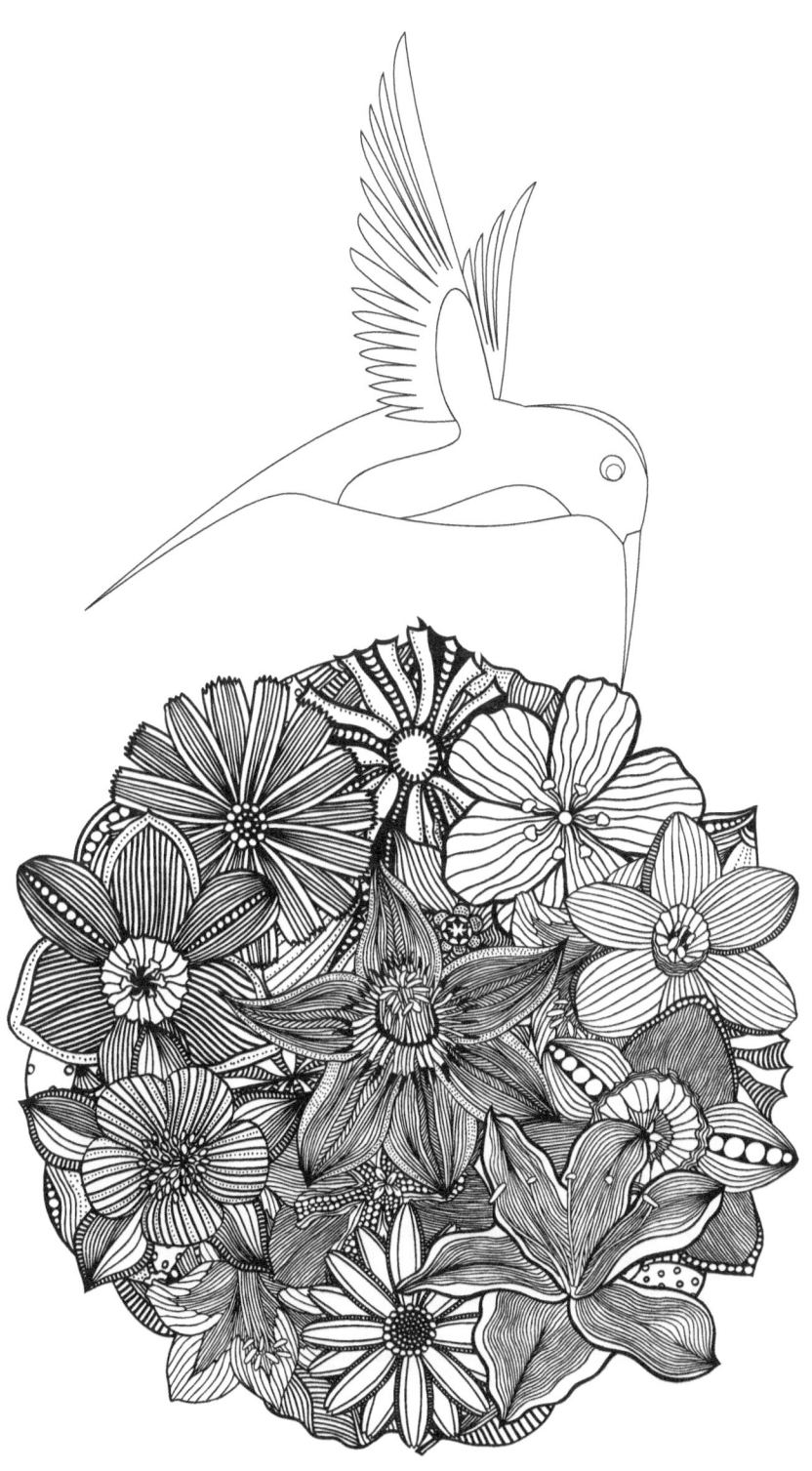

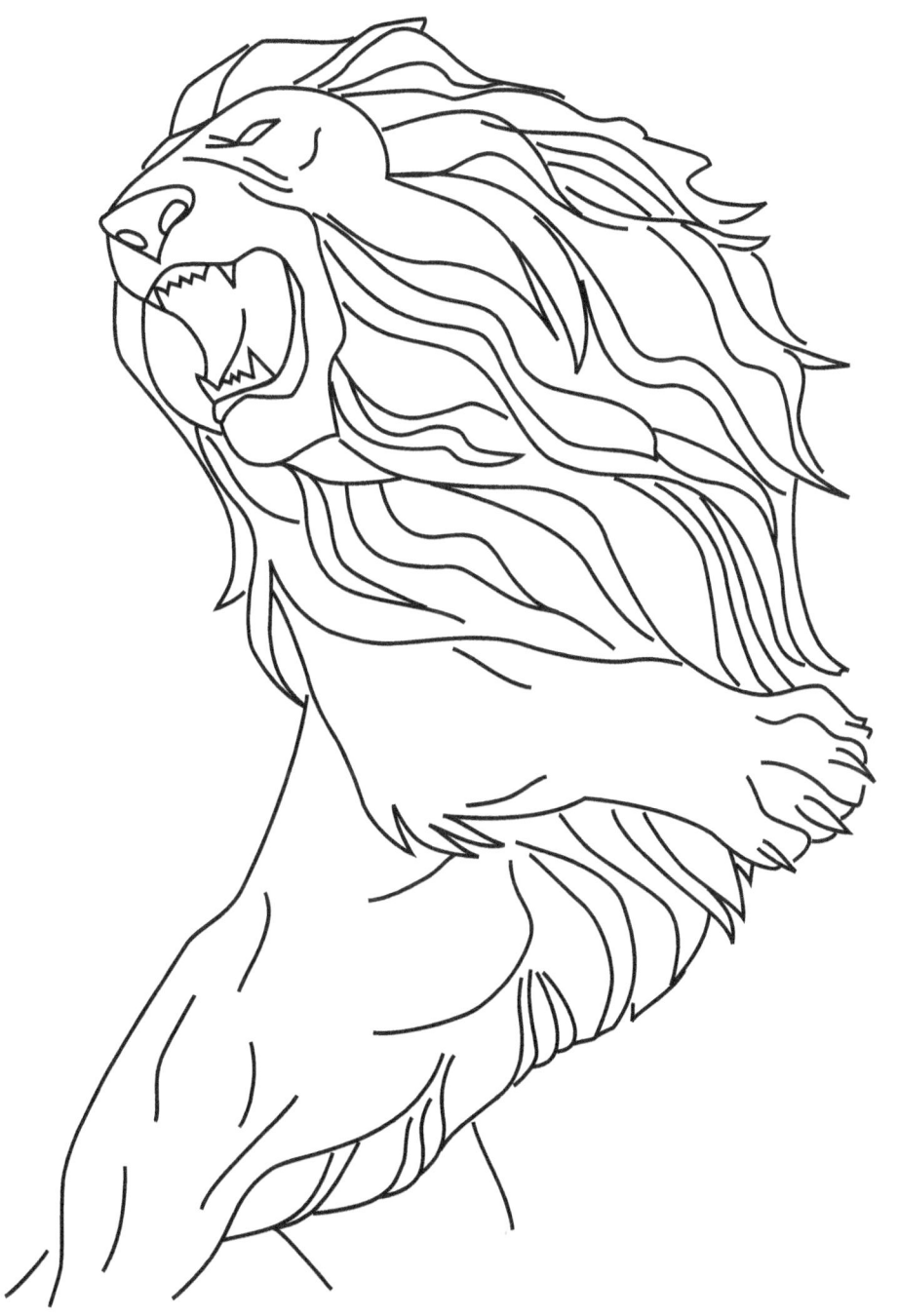

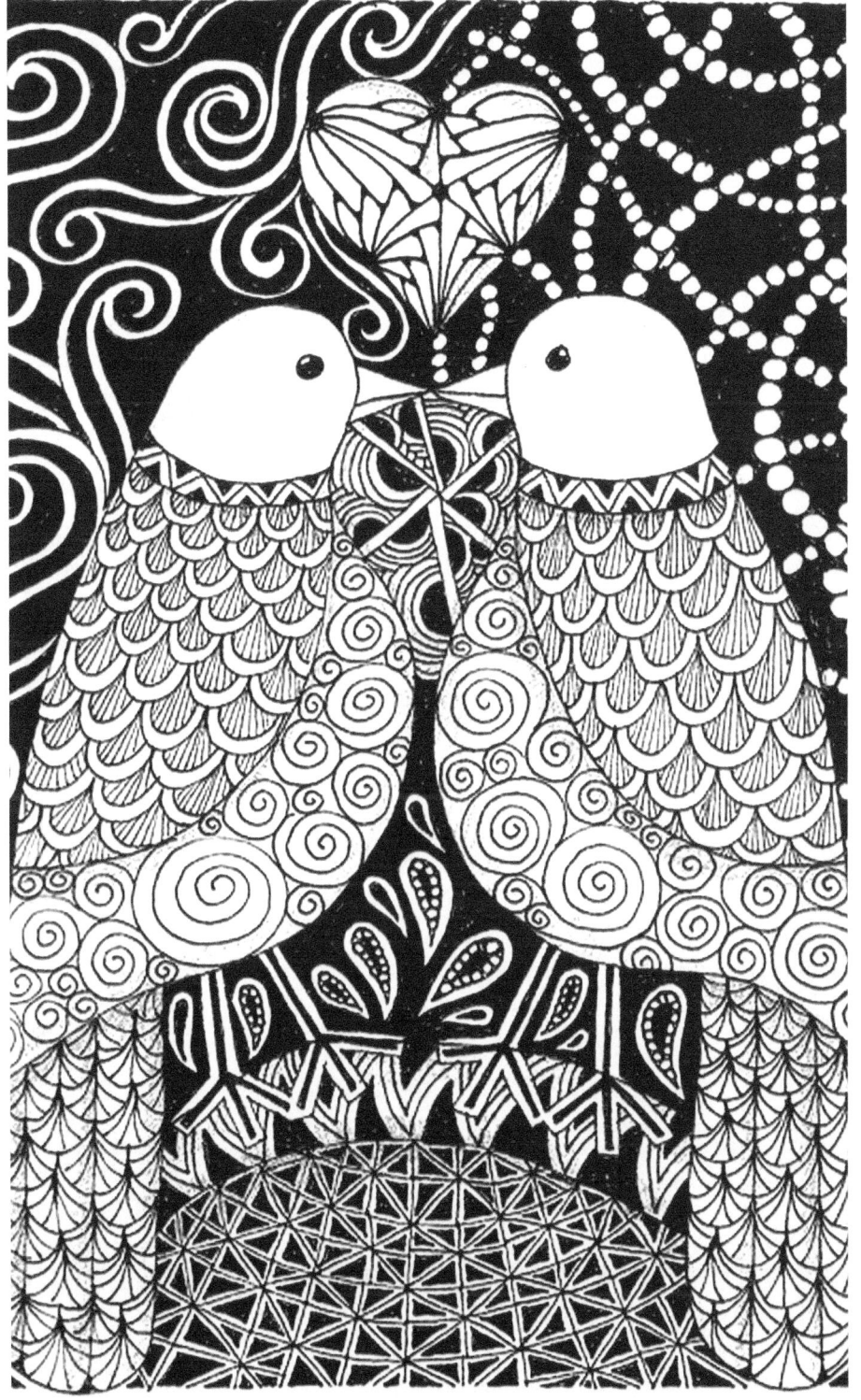

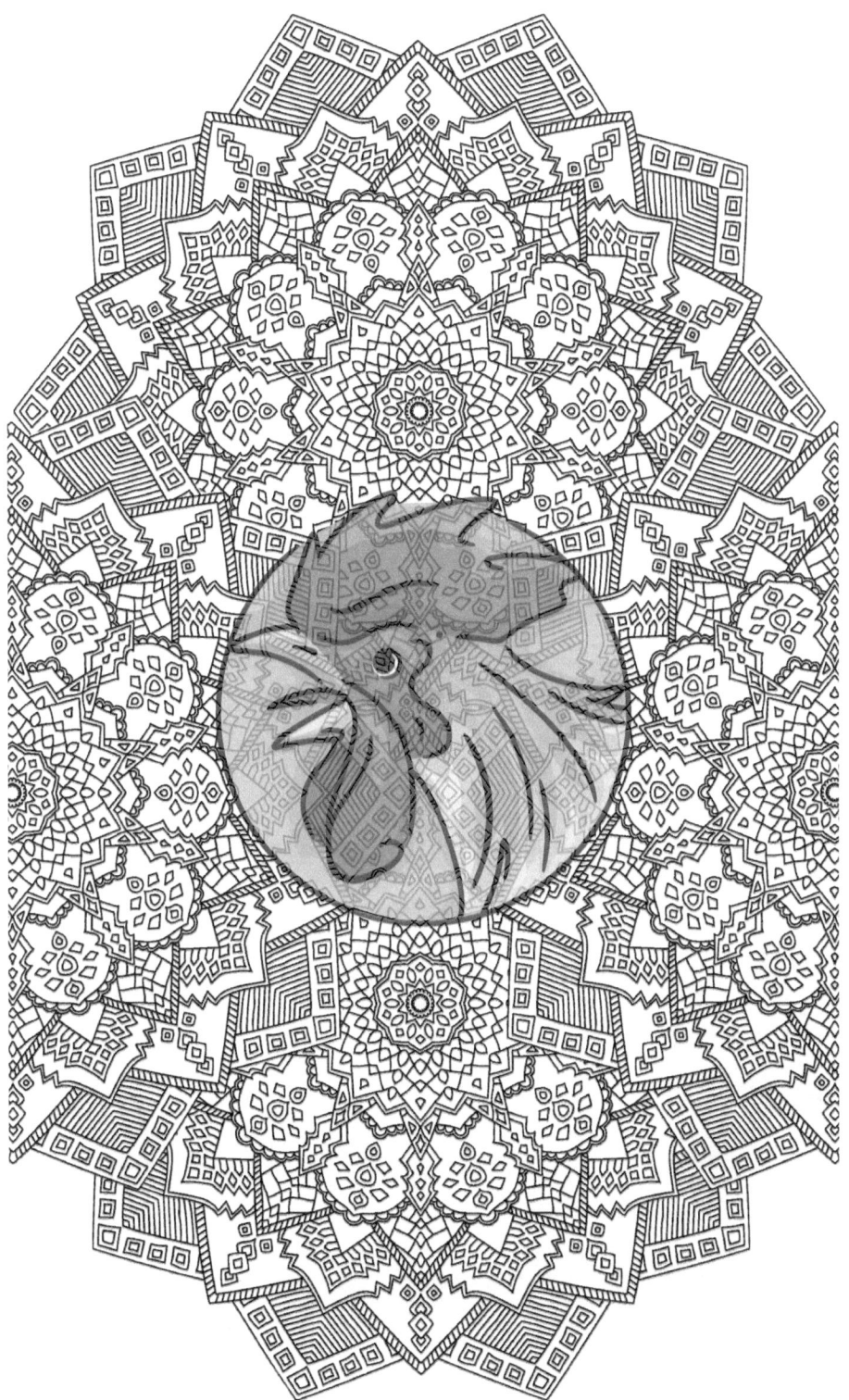

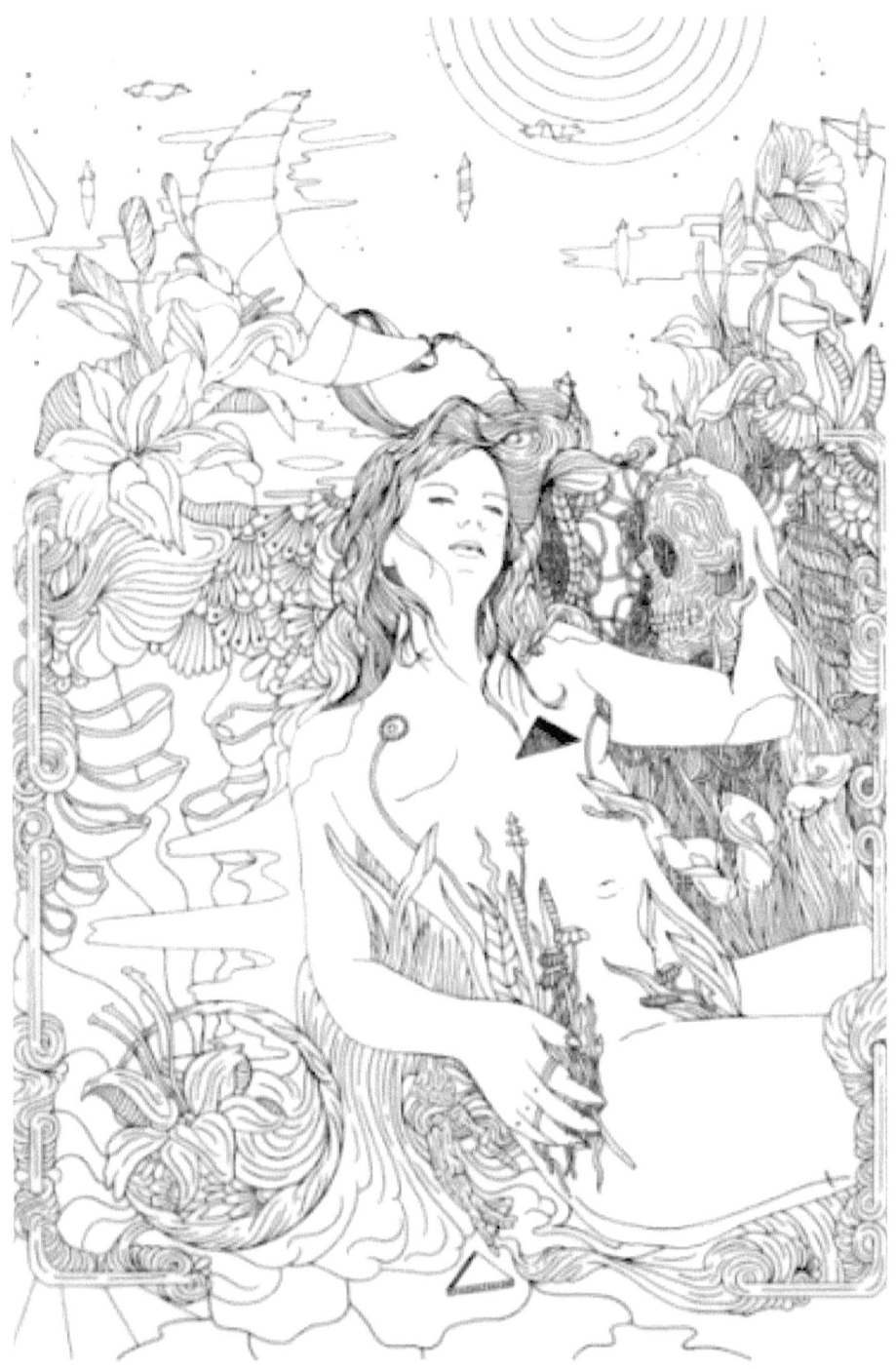

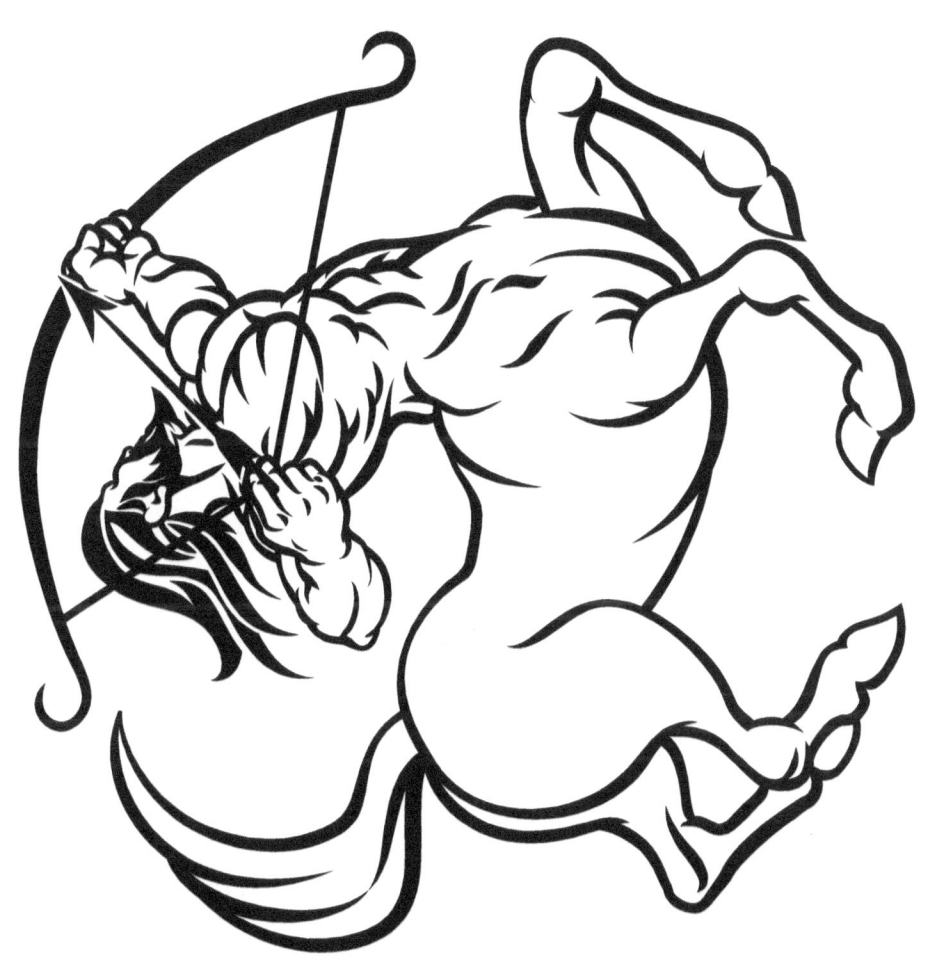

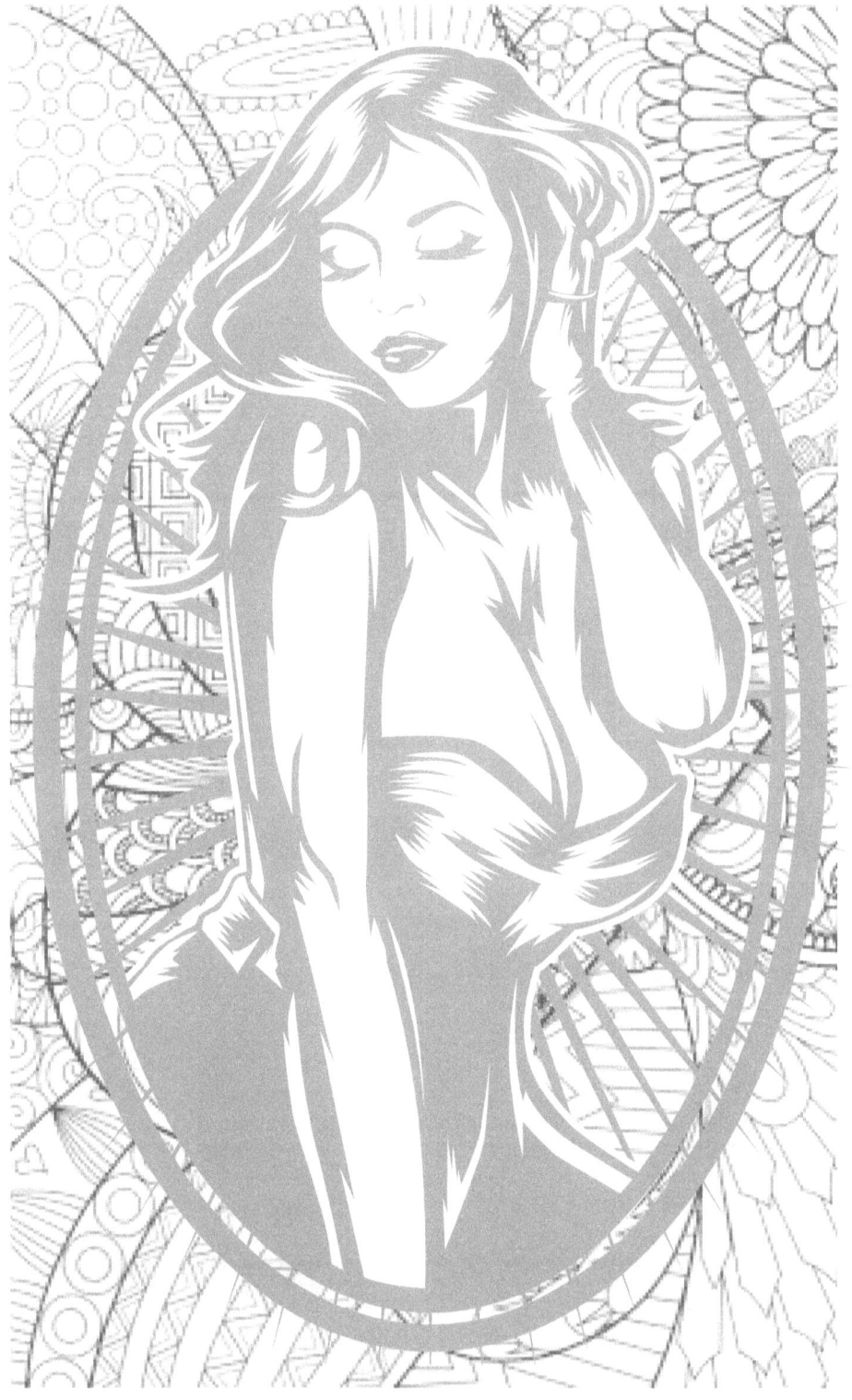

Thank you!

www.ingramcontent.com/pod-product-compliance
Lightning Source LLC
Chambersburg PA
CBHW021508210526
45463CB00002B/943